COUNTRY LIVING

Making & Displaying Quilts

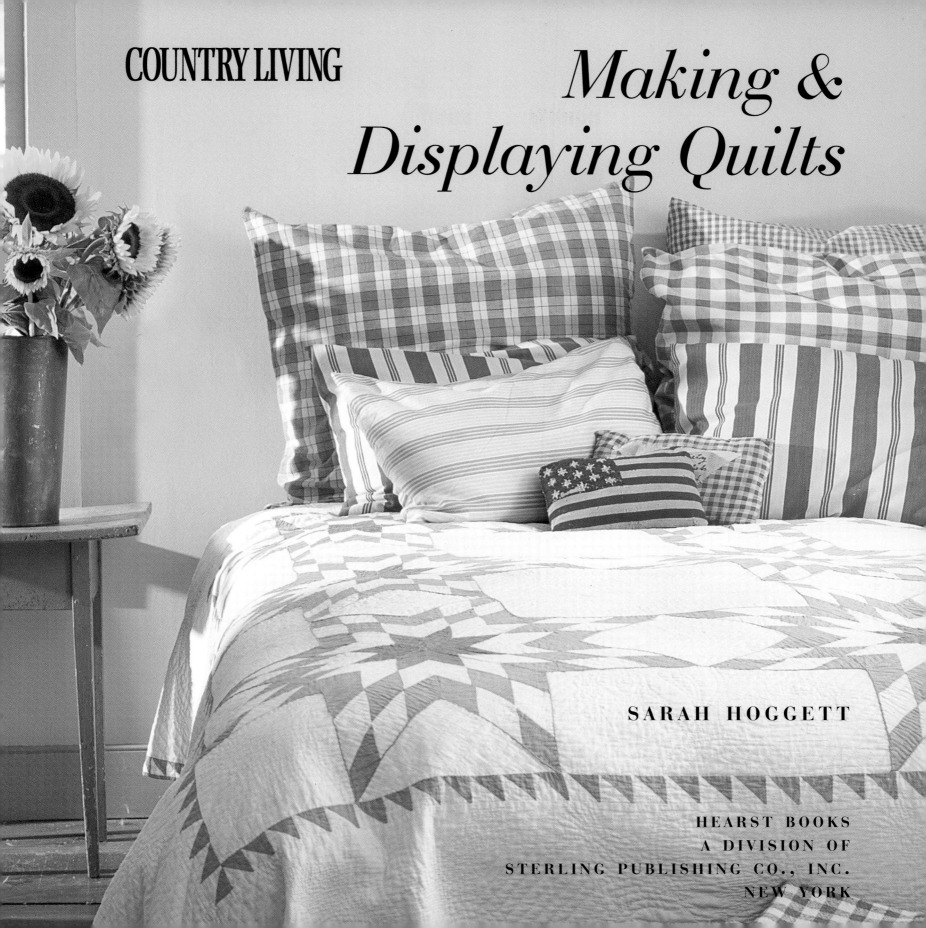

COUNTRY LIVING

Making & Displaying Quilts

SARAH HOGGETT

HEARST BOOKS
A DIVISION OF
STERLING PUBLISHING CO., INC.
NEW YORK

Library of Congress Cataloging-in-Publication Data

Hoggett, Sarah.

Country living making & displaying quilts / Sarah Hoggett.

p. cm.

ISBN 1-58816-273-7

1. Patchwork—Patterns. 2. Quilting—Patterns. 3. Patchwork quilts.

I. Title: Country living making and displaying quilts. II. Title.

TT835.H545 2003

746.46'041—dc21

2003006326

10 9 8 7 6 5 4 3 2 1

Published by Hearst Books
A Division of Sterling Publishing Co., Inc.
387 Park Avenue South, New York, N.Y. 10016

Country Living is a trademark owned by Hearst Magazines Property, Inc., in USA,
and Hearst Communications, Inc., in Canada. Hearst Books is a trademark owned by
Hearst Communications, Inc.

www.countryliving.com

Distributed in Canada by Sterling Publishing
c/o Canadian Manda Group, One Atlantic Avenue, Suite 105
Toronto, Ontario, Canada M6K 3E7
Distributed in Australia by Capricorn Link (Australia) Pty. Ltd.
P.O. Box 704, Windsor, NSW 2756 Australia

Printed in China

ISBN 1-58816-273-7

Designed by Christine Wood

The fabric quantities given in the projects are based on using fabrics that are 44" wide
and have been worked out using the most economical cutting plans possible. If you
are using fabric in a different width, or are unsure of your cutting skills, you may need
to adjust the quantities—your local quilt store should be able to advise you.

contents

foreword

Patchwork and quilting have long held a place of honor in American folk art. From being thrifty means of recycling old shirts and dresses to make warm bed linen for the long, cold nights of winter, quilts quickly became an artistic outlet for generations of women who had little or no formal training but who could, with nothing more than a needle and a pair of scissors, transform simple pieces of fabric into creations of beauty.

Today, interior decorators and even multinational manufacturers are waking up to the fact that vintage or reproduction quilts can do so much to enhance the personality of a room. Patchwork and quilting are more popular than ever before, with quilt stores and societies in every state and countless publications and websites devoted to the subject. Quilts themselves are as much at home in our great museums and galleries today as they would have been in Abe Lincoln's famed log cabin.

Country Living magazine has always celebrated the best of American design and *Making & Displaying Quilts* brings together some of the very finest quilts that we have encountered over the years. Whether you're an avid quilter yourself or simply enjoy looking at these superb pieces of textile art, I hope it will both inspire and inform you.

Nancy Mernit Soriano

Editor-in-Chief, *Country Living*

introduction: the beauty of quilts

Quilting is an intrinsic part of American history, which goes back to the days of the early pioneer settlers. Traditionally, women got together to make quilts in gatherings known as quilting bees, a tradition that is still strong today. A quilting bee fulfilled a practical and a social need: with rural dwellings scattered far apart, it was a rare chance for women to get together, catch up on news, and swap recipes and domestic tips. It gave people a much-needed break from everyday chores and bees were eagerly anticipated.

> "Thus the day was spent in friendly gossip as they quilted and rolled and talked and laughed . . . One might have learned in that instructive assembly how best to keep moths out of blankets; how to make fritters of Indian corn undistinguishable from oysters; how to bring up babies by hand; how to mend a cracked teapot; . . . how to make five yards of cloth answer the purpose of six; and how to put down the Democratic party."
>
> Description of a quilting bee from *The Minister's Wooing*,
> by Harriet Beecher Stowe

There can be few better descriptions of the quilting bee than the one here, written by Harriet Beecher Stowe in 1859. Each family would have made several quilt tops during the long winter months and quilting bees were a chance for the quilts to be completed before the next winter set in. As the saying goes, "many hands make light work." With a number of experienced stitchers working for several hours at a time, it was not unusual to finish a whole quilt in just one day. Everyone contributed in some form. The women worked on the quilts in shifts, with some sewing while others helped out in the kitchen. Even the children had their part to play, threading needles to keep the work in full swing. And in the evening when the men returned, the real festivities began with plenty to eat and drink, and perhaps even a square dance.

Quilting bees were often held to celebrate special occasions, such as comings of age (a young man would be given a freedom quilt for his twenty-first birthday), engagements, and weddings.

Traditionally, a girl was expected to piece twelve quilt tops for her dowry. However, largely because of the expense of actually constructing a quilt, the tops were not quilted—and so the quilting bee was tantamount to an official engagement announcement.

Since the 1970s there has been a huge revival of interest in quilting. Part of this interest, undoubtedly, stems from a desire to find out about the past: many of us own quilts that were made by our grandmothers, or even our great-grandmothers, and knowing something about these quilts (perhaps that they were made as a wedding gift, or to commemorate a dear friend or family member) provides us with a tangible link to previous generations. Above all, I think, we love quilts for their beauty. Many of our most stunning vintage quilts were made by women with little or no formal artistic training, yet they demonstrate an innate and awe-inspiring sense of color and design; their makers were by no means mathematical experts, but they were able to work out complex patterns and cut and sew fabric with almost unbelievable precision. And today's quilters are raising quilting to new heights, with wonderfully inventive pieces that can only be described as textile art.

People sometimes get confused about the difference between patchwork and quilting. Think of a quilt as a kind of fabric sandwich. It consists of three layers—the top, the batting (a layer of warm material used as a filling), and the backing fabric. Strictly speaking, the word *quilting* means stitching through all three layers of a quilt to hold them together, although it is also used as a more general term to mean the whole process of making a quilt.

Patchwork is a method of making a large piece of fabric by stitching smaller pieces (patches) together—usually in a predetermined pattern, although they can be stitched randomly, as in crazy patchwork. Appliqué is the term used to describe the process of stitching one piece of fabric on top of another—usually a cutout decorative motif on top of a background fabric. (The term originates from the French word, *appliquer*, which literally means, to apply.) Patchwork and appliqué are both techniques that you can

BELOW: CLASSIC COLORS
A traditional, mid-19th century appliqué quilt in red and green.

use to make the decorative top of the quilt: they are both aspects of the wider topic of quilting. Depending on how the top of the quilt is to be constructed, you can have a patchwork quilt, or an appliqué quilt. There are also various other types of quilt, such as trapunto or corded quilts (see page 11 for more information).

Making & Displaying Quilts offers both an aesthetic and a practical introduction to quilting. Superb photographs of both old and new quilts provide both inspiration and practical advice on how to display quilts, while "Get the Look" features show you how to use quilts to create particular styles of decorating. Throughout, you will find "Quilting Tradition" features that look at specific types of quilts or patterns in more

detail. Each chapter ends with projects, most of which are suitable for beginners and intermediate quilters. The quantities are based on fabrics that are 44" wide. If you are using a different width, or are unsure of your cutting skills, you may need to adjust the quantities—your local quilt store can advise you. The book ends with a "Quilting know-how" section that gives the technical information you need to complete the projects and also serves as a quick-and-easy refresher course for people who have done some patchwork and quilting already.

Making & Displaying Quilts is both a practical introduction to the traditional art of quiltmaking and a tribute to quiltmakers past and present. They have left us a rich and inspiring legacy, and I hope that this book does them justice.

Sarah Hoggett

BELOW: STARS AND STRIPES This striking quilt combines a strip-pieced border and star blocks with appliquéd hearts. The color combination of red, brown, and cream are restrained but effective.

glossary of terms

Words in *italic* refer to other entries in the glossary.

APPLIQUÉ: the process of stitching one piece of fabric on top of another (usually a decorative cutout motif onto a background fabric).

BACKING: the layer of fabric that forms the back of a quilt.

BATTING: soft, padded material used as the middle layer of a quilt to provide warmth. It is usually synthetic, but cotton batting and blends of cotton and polyester are also available. Batting is available in different weights. In the United Kingdom, it is known as wadding.

BLOCK: the basic unit that makes up a patchwork design. A number of identical blocks may be made to form the quilt top; the overall look of the quilt depends on the choice of *setting*.

FAT QUARTER: one-quarter of a yard of fabric, made by cutting a half yard in half again vertically. Most quilting shops will do this. The piece is approximately 18" x 22". Cutting in this way allows you to produce larger blocks than from a standard quarter yard (9" x 44").

PATCHWORK: the technique of stitching together small pieces of fabric to make a larger one.

QUILTING: stitching through the top, *batting*, and *backing* of a quilt to hold the layers together. In hand quilting, tiny running stitches are normally used.

   CORDED QUILTING: a quilting technique in which two layers of fabric are sewn together using parallel lines of running stitch, creating a channel. Cord is then threaded through, creating a raised effect.

ECHO QUILTING: a style of quilting in which the quilting stitches run close to the inside or outside edges of a *patchwork* or *appliqué* piece, echoing its shape.

MEANDER QUILTING: a style of machine quilting that follows no pre-marked pattern but is stitched randomly over the piece, creating dense texture.

OUTLINE QUILTING: a style of quilting in which the line of stitching is positioned around a block or *appliqué* piece.

QUILTING IN THE DITCH: a style of quilting in which the quilting stitches are in or very close to the seam lines.

TIED: a quilting technique in which yarn or thread is taken through all three layers of a quilt and back up to the top again, and tied in a knot to hold the layers together.

TRAPUNTO: a technique similar to *corded quilting*, with certain areas being stuffed with small pieces of *batting* from the wrong side, so that the design stands out in relief.

SASHING: strips of fabric sewn between the *blocks* of a quilt top. Sashing can run both vertically and horizontally.

SETTING: the way in which the various parts of a quilt top are arranged.

   EDGE TO EDGE: setting the *blocks* of a quilt top side by side, with no *sashing* separating them.

   ON POINT: rotating the *blocks* of a quilt top through 90° so that they form a diamond shape rather than a square.

   PIECED AND PLAIN SET: alternating pieced *blocks* with solid-colored blocks the same size.

CHAPTER ONE

color

Color is one of the most exciting
aspects of quilting. Although careful
planning is essential and there
are general guidelines to follow,
don't be afraid to experiment
with unusual combinations. The
results can be spectacular.

the fascination of color

Take a look at any display of quilts, antique or modern, and what is the first thing that strikes you? Think of traditional Amish designs with their surprisingly bright blues and pinks, or Log Cabin quilts in which the transition from light to dark fabrics is so subtle that it almost seems as if a cloud is hovering overhead and casting its shadow, or mid-19th century designs in Turkey red fabric on a white background: the chances are that it's the color that initially attracts your eye.

"Brama Lincoln White was engaged to William French, . . . the first Sunday in July, and the very next week her mother, Mrs. Harrison White, sent out invite' tions to a quilting bee."

A Quilting Bee in Our Village,
Mary Eleanor Wilkins Freeman

Quilt colors can also help us date quilts. For example, we think of red and white, and blue and white, as being classic color combinations for quilts, but it wasn't until the middle of the nineteenth century that manufacturers were first able to produce colorfast dyes in these colors. We can be fairly certain that quilts in these colorways date from after 1850. In the early twentieth century, colors became brighter and cheerier, with more depth; the new aniline dyes of that time also meant that colors were less fugitive than they had been in the past.

Playing with color is one of the most fascinating and enjoyable aspects of quilting, and studying the work of other quilters is a great starting point for learning what works and what doesn't. It will also give you lots of ideas for unusual color and fabric combinations. But if you need a little more help, here are some general guidelines.

FAR RIGHT: SMALL PATTERNS
This Dresden Plate quilt uses scraps of 1930s-style fabrics in small patterns. Although the "plates" look very busy, the restful peppermint-green background fabric holds the design together.

ABOVE: COLOR INSPIRATION
Why not look to the natural world for guidance when it comes to choosing colors?

RIGHT: ADDITIONAL TEXTURES
Upholstery fabrics in soft, harmonious shades, piled in a painted woven basket, are a great way of bringing additional color, as well as textures, into your decorating scheme.

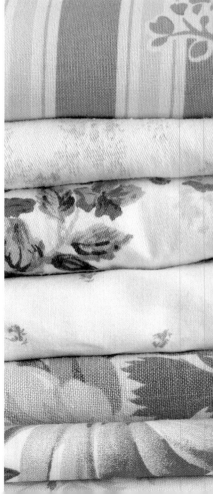

combining colors

You're probably already familiar with most of the basic terminology of color theory, but here's a quick refresher course. There are three primary colors—red, yellow, and blue—from which all other colors can be made. Mix two primaries together and you get a secondary color—so red mixed with yellow gives orange, red mixed with blue gives purple, and so on. Colors that fall between the primaries and secondaries are known as intermediates.

Analogous, or harmonious, colors are ones that are next to each other on the color wheel—for example, orange shading through rich yellow to a paler yellow. Analogous colors are virtually guaranteed to look good together, but the mood you create depends on whether you use purely primary colors (which can look very vibrant and "loud") or introduce some of the intermediate shades, which generally give a more restful, calming result.

Complementary colors are opposite one another on the color wheel: red and green are complementaries, as are blue and orange. Using a color with its complementary makes it appear more intense. This is called a contrasting color scheme, and it can be used to create a very dramatic, bold quilt.

In quilting there is also another type of contrasting color scheme, and that is one that is based on value, rather than color. Value means the relative darkness or lightness of a color, and strongly contrasting values—a pale color such as white or cream with dark shades such as red, blue, or brown—always have great impact, particularly when only two colors are involved. The classic combinations of red and white, or blue and white, are examples of contrasting color schemes.

LEFT: CONTRASTING COLORS
Two very traditional quilts in the same contrasting color scheme of green and cream: on the left, Robbing Peter to Pay Paul, and on the right, Maple Leaves.

BELOW: STYLISH ACCESSORIES
Shaker-style boxes echo the colors used in the quilts and suit the simplicity of the décor.

get the look: neutral sophistication

The pale walls, beige sofa and foreground armchair, and coffee-and-cream checked rug provide a neutral backdrop that allows the stronger colors of the patchwork quilts to stand out dramatically.

The dark wood and strong shapes of the grandfather clock, lamp base, and statue also have strong visual impact, as does the leather armchair.

Every object counts in this room. The few ornaments are big and bold and help to give an overall impression of space and lack of clutter.

LEFT: NEUTRAL BACKGROUNDS
The quilts draped over the chair are a testament to the maker's sense of design. Both are very simple patterns—one a bold red star on a neutral background, and the other squares of colorful checked fabric on plain calico.

Provided the contrast in value is strong enough, two-color schemes look very crisp and clean. A white background makes the other color look very rich and saturated, while a black one will emphasize the shape of any motif placed on it and make the color glow. When the contrast in value is very extreme (black and white, for instance), a kind of optical illusion results, so that it's hard to tell which is the background color and which the foreground, or whether you're looking at positive or negative shapes. This can have great graphic impact—but it can also be a little hard on the eye.

Last but not least, think about whether colors look warm or cool, as this also affects mood. As a general rule, reds, oranges, and yellows are described as warm, while blues tend to be cool.

using patterned and multicolored fabrics

Of course, fabrics come in all sort of patterns and color combinations, not just as solid colors—and your choice of fabric is one of the things that will make each piece unique. Even if you begin quilting by using scraps of fabric left over from other projects, once the bug bites you'll find yourself buying fabrics specifically for quilting, in the certain knowledge that they'll come in useful one day even if you don't yet know exactly what you'll do with them.

For dedicated quilters, fabric stores have got to be among the most seductive locations on earth. Row upon row of dressweight cottons in every color of the rainbow, with each color graded from light to dark; checks and stripes; dainty florals; bold ethnic prints; and printed

LEFT: WARM COLORS
Whoever put together this combination has a wonderful sense of color harmony: yellow, orange, and red are close together in the color spectrum—and, because they are all "warm" colors, the room has a feeling of great coziness.

RIGHT: COOL CONTRAST
The small touch of blue in the stars-and-stripes pillow introduces a contrasting "cool" color that balances the whole display.

motifs on virtually every subject under the sun, from eighteenth-century-style toiles de Jouy to teddy bears and Christmas cherubs: a patchworker's paradise!

It's tempting to buy indiscriminately, snatching up every fabric that catches your eye, sending your credit cards into meltdown mode, and filling every closet in the house with fat quarters and bolts of cotton. But even if you have the money and the space, this isn't necessarily going to set you on the road to creating stunning quilts. So what should you look for?

"So I want to take lessons in sewing of her. She works so beautifully, and it is a useful thing, you know, and I ought to be a good needlewoman as well as housekeeper, oughtn't I?"

From *Eight Cousins* by Louisa May Alcott

A good range of solid colors is essential, particularly if your chosen pattern includes large, bold shapes (see the two-color Evening Star pattern on pages 38–41, for example). Most of all, however, make sure that you have a good range of values from light to dark: this is one of the most important considerations when you are planning a quilt, as many patterns rely for their impact on the way in which light and dark fabrics are positioned. The same pattern can take on a completely different feel when it is made in different values.

Dark fabrics tend to look as if they are receding while light ones appear to advance, and so light and dark values create depth—particularly in patterns that are based on optical illusions, such as the Tumbling Blocks quilt on pages 76–77, where the careful placement of light, medium, and dark values creates a three-dimensional effect.

(Continued on page 26)

RIGHT: CLASSIC CONTRAST
Not only are red and white a striking combination of contrasting colors, but the neat hand stitching on this quilt is a work of art in its own right.

get the look: contemporary chic

A perfect balance of old and new, of country charm and chic sophistication.

The key is to decide on the most important decorative feature—the wonderful red and white Churn Dash quilt—and make sure nothing else is allowed to dominate it.

Start with color. Carefully placed splashes of red (the pillow edges, and berry-filled glass vase) echo the colors of the quilt and offset the large expanses of white. Elsewhere, gold detailing adds just a hint of opulence.

Then think about textures. Introduce contrasts of shape and texture to keep the room from looking bland. The lilies provide a sculptural shape, as well as being beautifully scented.

LEFT: SASHING
The blocks on the redwork quilt draped over the end of the daybed are separated by sashing in the same shade as the thread. The quilt layers are held together by means of decorative ties.

RIGHT: PRINTED BORDER
All the blocks in these quilts are beautifully embroidered, but it is less common to find printed fabric borders like the one around the center block: most redwork blocks are embroidered on a solid white background.

FAR RIGHT: TYPICAL MOTIFS
A selection of the kind of motifs commonly found in redwork blocks.

Quilting tradition: redwork

Redwork—a type of outline embroidery worked in red cotton thread on a white linen or cotton background, usually in stem stitch— became hugely popular after a bright red, colorfast dye came into production around the middle of the nineteenth century. By the late nineteenth century, the craze had spread to bedcovers and quilts and was a standard way for young girls to practice their needlework skills.

Redwork reached its peak of popularity between about 1900 and 1920, with ladies' magazines and newspapers producing countless patterns. Pre-printed muslin squares packaged with enough embroidery floss to make the design were also widely sold by chain stores such as Woolworths. They cost just one cent—and so the squares came to be known as "Penny Squares."

Penny squares typically measured 6 to 10 inches. When enough blocks had been embroidered, they could be sewn together into quilts. Feather or cross stitch were often used to cover the seam lines, and later quilts sometimes featured red sashing.

The huge range of motifs included biblical tales, children's stories, animals, birds, flowers, monograms, and even such newsworthy events as the death of Jumbo, Phineas Barnum's circus elephant, in 1885. Political figures, too, were immortalized in Turkey red thread: after President McKinley's assassination at the Pan American Exposition in 1901, a redwork pattern appeared featuring his profile and the words, "Our Martyred President." With the current revival of interest in redwork, such commemorative pieces are now particularly collectible.

However, a whole quilt pieced from solid colors can sometimes look a little bland. Small-scale prints—for example, tiny polka dots or sprigs of flowers on a single-colored background—look solid from a distance, but will add much-needed sparkle and life to your pattern. If you try an arrangement of fabrics for a quilt and find that it looks dull, try substituting a small print for a solid color: it can make the world of difference. Small-scale stripes and checks, too, can liven up patterns considerably if they are carefully positioned.

Medium- and large-scale prints should be used with caution: if you use a large number in one design, it will look too busy and the eye will have nowhere to rest. With large-scale prints, you may find that you can cut out a small part of the pattern to use as a motif.

choosing colors: decision time . . .

So you've decided to make the quilt, ransacked your fabric stash to see what goodies it contains, and realized you need to go shopping (again). What next? Your choice of colors and fabrics is probably the most important decision you make when constructing a quilt and it can be quite a nerve-wracking experience. After all, if you're making a quilt for a double bed, you may have to spend a considerable

LEFT: PATTERN POWER
The visual energy of this lovely quilt comes not only from the dynamic color contrasts, but also from the tiny-patterned black and green fabric squares that alternate with the appliquéd blocks.

RIGHT: MIXING PATTERNS
Don't be afraid to mix prints: if you stick to harmonious colors and think about the scale, then florals, checks, solids, and stripes can all work well together.

amount of money on fabric, especially for a complex pattern, so you want to be as sure as you can that it's going to look right.

A good starting point is to decide on the mood you want to create. Do you want a soft, romantic feel (soft pastels and pretty florals, perhaps), a rustic look (neutral colors might be a good choice of background fabric, balanced with checks or other small-patterned materials), or something that would work in a sophisticated, ultramodern apartment? Is it for a child's room or an adult's? If you're making it as a gift, maybe you can incorporate the recipient's favorite colors, or pieces of fabric from a much-loved dress that they no longer wear. Asking yourself questions like these will help you to narrow down your options.

Then, take small pieces of the fabrics you're thinking of using, jumble them all up, and then scatter them randomly on a table or floor; if any one of them clashes with any of the others, discard it. And if you're considering a pattern that's based on a repeating block, why not buy a small amount of fabric and make just one block before you embark on the rest of the quilt?

Ultimately, however, remember that color is a very personal choice. The pointers mentioned above are just guidelines, not hard and fast rules. By all means, experiment and look at what other quilters have created, but the final decision is yours and yours alone. If you like it, then it works!

> "The PATCHWORK QUILT! . . . a miscellaneous collection of odd bits and ends of calico . . . each of which is a key to some painful or pleasant remembrance . . ."
>
> "The Patchwork Quilt," *The Lowell Offering*, 1842

BELOW: TEAMING COLOR WITH PATTERN
Big, bold motifs combine with delicate colors to produce a pretty, subtle quilt.

RIGHT: BUTTERFLIES
This stylized but very effective butterflies quilt combines appliqué with simple embroidery. Judging by the fresh but soft colors and the style of the small-patterned prints, it probably dates from the 1930s.

get the look:
1950s retro

Retro-style floral patterns are very much in vogue, but having lots of them in a room can make the décor scheme look very busy. Counteract this by placing a throw in a solid color over the foot of the bed, picking out one of your favorite colors in the quilt fabrics.

When choosing your colors, think about the existing décor of the room—you may find inspiration for your quilt. On the other hand, your choice of quilt fabrics may inspire you to redecorate the room!

Boldly striped rugs also help to balance the tiny patterns of the quilt fabrics.

Paint the metal bedstead in a contrasting period color: here, the fresh green offsets the dominant pink shades of the quilt perfectly.

Small botanical prints on the shelf pick up the overall color scheme and enhance its soft, feminine quality.

Quilting tradition: star quilts

Star patterns have appeared on pieced and appliquéd quilts since the very early days of quilting in the eighteenth century. As a result, there are probably more kinds of star quilts than any other type of patchwork design: in fact, quilt scholars have documented no less than 150 different star patterns.

There are four-pointed stars, six-pointed stars, and eight-pointed stars. There are stars that are pieced from simple squares and triangles and stars like the Feathered Star, shown opposite, that are masterpieces of precision piecing. There are graphic-looking single-color stars on dark backgrounds that look as if they're twinkling in the night sky and stars pieced from myriad tiny diamond shapes that radiate outward in kaleidoscopic explosions of color. There are

stars pieced from random scraps and stars in which the choice of color and fabric is painstakingly planned down to the very last detail.

The names are as varied as the designs. Some, such as Blazing Star and Sawtooth Star, are purely descriptive. Others, such as Star of Bethlehem, have biblical significance. Still others bear the names of specific individuals, such as the LeMoyne Star, named for the two French brothers who are reputed to have founded the city of New Orleans in the early eighteenth century. There are stars associated with particular states—Ohio Star, and Lone Star (symbol of the State of Texas). And there are even a number of star-shaped patterns that don't carry the name of star, such as Card Trick. Even after two hundred years, the popularity of the motif shows no sign of fading.

LEFT: DIAMOND STAR
One of the simplest star designs, this pattern is made using the paper-piecing method (see page 142) to stitch eight yellow diamonds into a star. Blue corner squares and a triangle in the center of each edge complete the block.

RIGHT: PRIMARY COLORS
Blue and yellow are a popular, effective color combination. The decorative yellow ties used to hold the three layers of this Feathered Star quilt together carry through the color theme and enliven the dark blue background.

classic color combination: robbing Peter to pay Paul

This strikingly modern-looking design takes its name from the fact that pieces are "borrowed" from one block and used in another. When several blocks are pieced together, a secondary pattern of two-color circles emerges.

Two colors are normally used for this type of design, although it is possible to build up complex and intriguing patterns using more colors. As in so many other quilting designs, it is the contrast of light and dark and the interplay of negative and positive shapes that make this pattern so dramatic. The greater the tonal contrast, the stronger the effect—and so red and white, as used here, has tremendous graphic impact.

With all curved designs, make sure you align the pieces correctly and do not stretch the fabric (see page 141). Pinning the pieces before you stitch them might seem like a time-consuming process, but it is time well spent. It is also worth checking the reverse from time to time as you stitch, to make sure that your stitches are on the marked line.

LEFT: CIRCULAR SPLENDOR
Careful piecing is the key to success in this design: the circles must match up properly or the effect will be ruined.

33

robbing Peter to pay Paul

Finished size:
approx. 63" x 81"

Block size: 9"

Number of blocks: 63

You will need:

- 3½ yds. red fabric, *plus*
  ½ yd. red fabric to make binding
- 3½ yds. white fabric
- 5 yds. fabric for backing
- 5 yds. of 2-oz. batting
- Matching sewing and quilting threads

All fabrics should be 44" wide.

RED QUILTING ON WHITE FABRIC
Using red thread on white fabric provides visual interest. The straight lines of quilting stitches also balance the curves of the patchwork pieces.

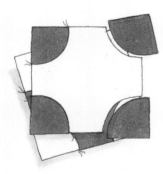

1 Using the templates on page 150, cut out one A piece in one color and four B pieces in the other color. Taking ¼" seam allowances, stitch each B piece to one curved side of piece A, taking care to avoid stretching the curves. Make 32 blocks that have red as the main color, and 31 that have white as the main color.

2 Starting with a block that has red as the main color and alternating colors, stitch together seven blocks to make a horizontal row. For the next row, start with a block that has white as the main piece. Continue until you have completed nine rows.

3 Stitch the horizontal rows together to complete the top.

4 Assemble the quilt layers, pin, and baste. Mark the quilt with diagonal lines and quilt in red thread.

5 Add a single binding in red fabric (see pages 148–149).

blue and white checkerboard

Blue and white are a classic color combination, and this crisp checkerboard design is both graphic and elegant. This quilt is strip-pieced, but then the top is rotated so that the squares are "on point" and look like diamonds.

LEFT: CRISP CONTRASTS
Simply pieced designs like this checkerboard will work well in almost any interior, from a modern apartment to a rustic farmstead.

You will need:
- 1½ yds. white fabric
- 2 yds. blue fabric
- 2 yds. of 2-oz. batting
- 2 yds. fabric for backing
- Matching sewing and quilting threads

All fabrics should be 44" wide.

Finished size: approx. 38" x 63"

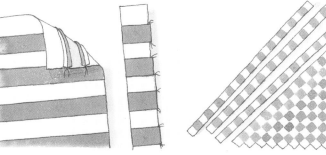

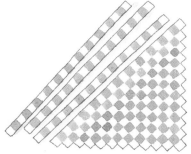

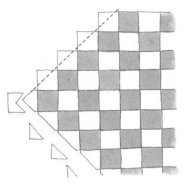

4 Cut the strips for the borders: 2" wide for the inner blue border, 2½" for the white border, and 4½" for the outer blue border. Taking ¼" seams, strip-piece the borders. Join the borders to the quilt top using the "top and tail" technique (see page 143).

1 Reserve 42" of blue and 18" of white for borders. Cut the remainder into 2"-wide strips. Taking a ¼" seam allowance and starting with white, stitch them together, alternating the fabrics and stitching the seams in opposite directions. Cut the pieced units into 2"-wide strips.

2 Referring to the diagram above, work out how many squares you need in each row of the quilt. Unpick seams where necessary to get the right number. Stitch the rows together, taking a ¼" seam. Press each seam to one side.

3 Rotate the quilt top through 45° and mark out the rectangle of the finished quilt top. Trim off the excess white fabric, remembering to allow ¼" for the seam.

5 Assemble the quilt layers, pin, and baste. Quilt "in the ditch" (see page 147). Make a fold-finish (see page 148) around the outside edge.

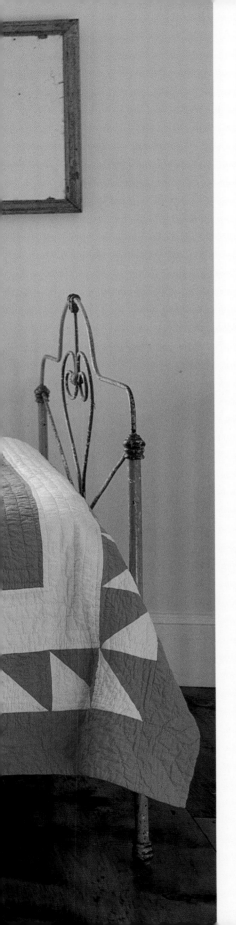

"One trade in all its branches, domestic
or otherwise, is likely to remain principally
our own—the use of the needle . . . truly,
no one but ourselves can tell what the
needle is to us women . . ."

A Woman's Thoughts About Women, Dinah Maria Mulock (1858)

two-color evening star

This beautiful star, which is made from large pieces in a single color,
is one of the simplest of all star patterns to make. Because the pieces
are so big, it is a very quick and easy design to piece: there are no
awkward curves or complex points to deal with, so everything can be
done by machine.

The color combination, too, is simple but extremely effective and
relies on strong contrast. A huge, rich orange star occupies the whole
of the center of the quilt, with the same color repeated in two jagged
sawtooth borders, while the background is a soothing pale cream.
Boldly shaped patterns such as this tend to work best in mid- or
dark tones on a pale, neutral background, which allows the design to
stand out dramatically.

Orange is a very warm, dynamic color and a quilt like this one
will impart a great sense of energy to any room in which it is
displayed. Make it the dominant feature of the room and be sure
to keep ornaments or other decorative items to a minimum so as not
to detract from the quilt itself.

LEFT: BOLD AND BRIGHT
This quilt cries out for a
simple, uncluttered setting
that will allow you to show it
off to its full advantage.

two-color evening star

Finished size: 85" x 85"
Central star block:
35" square

You will need:

FOR THE CENTRAL STAR:
● ¾ yd. cream fabric
● ¾ yd. orange fabric

FOR THE SAWTOOTH BORDERS:
● 1¼ yds. cream fabric
● 1¼ yds. orange fabric

FOR THE SOLID BORDERS:
● 2½ yds. orange fabric
● 1½ yds. cream fabric

TO COMPLETE THE QUILT:
● 7¾ yds. fabric for backing
● 7¾ yds. 2-oz. batting
● Matching sewing and quilting thread
All fabrics should be 44" wide.

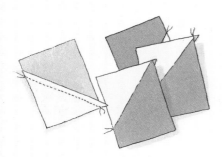

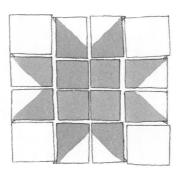

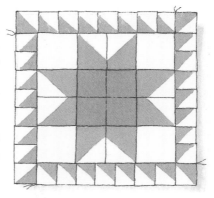

1 First make the central star. Trace the patterns on page 151 adding a ¼" seam allowance all around on each piece. Cut out four orange A pieces, then turn the pattern over and cut another four mirror-image pieces. Cut out four white B pieces, then turn the pattern over, as before, and cut four more pieces. Stitch together in four pieced rectangles, as shown in the illustration.

2 Cut four 8" orange squares and stitch them together to form the center. Position the pieced rectangles around it as in the diagram above; add corner 10½" cream squares, and piece together.

3 To make the inner sawtooth border, cut sixteen 5⅞" squares in each color. Cut each square in half diagonally and re-piece as a two-color patch. Assemble four strips of eight pieced squares each, making sure that, when the borders are in position, orange triangles run around the edge of the central square.

4 Using the "top and tail" method (see page 143) and taking a ¼" seam, attach a 5½" cream border followed by a 5½" orange border.

5 Make another sawtooth border, as in Step 3, from 28 5⅞" squares in each color. Finally, attach another 5½" orange border.

The quilting (straight lines on the plain borders and outline quilting on the sawtooth borders) is simple and subtle, but it adds much-needed texture to large areas of solid color.

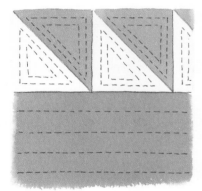

6 Assemble the quilt layers, pin, and baste. Echo quilt the central star and outline quilt all the triangles in the pieced borders (see page 147). Quilt the plain inner borders with evenly spaced straight lines and the plain outer border with curved lines or any other quilting motif of your choice. Make a fold-finish (see page 148).

matching tones: butterflies at the crossroads

Quilt patterns have such wonderfully evocative names. Here, butterflies made from pieced triangle and square patches flutter around a "crossroads" created by strips of sashing. Normally this block would be assembled as a straightforward five-patch. In this instance, however, the "crossroads" sashing that runs vertically and horizontally through the center of the block is narrower than the individual patches, and this has the effect of making the "butterflies" more prominent.

". . . Piecin' a quilt's like livin' a life. . ."

Eliza Calvert Hall

The same design worked as a four-patch without the sashing is known as Bear's Paw—and looking at it one can almost see with the mind's eye a grizzly bear, its four feet planted squarely on the ground, sniffing the air in search of food.

This particular quilt exploits color contrasts to great effect. The butterflies are pieced from dark, small-patterned browns and blues, and placing them on cream fabric gives the piece a lovely, airy feel. The blocks are then separated by vibrant red sashing, which creates a dynamic contrast to the blues and browns. The tonal values of the sashing and the dark fabrics used in the blocks are similar, and this also helps to tie the whole quilt together visually.

LEFT: PATRIOTIC COLORS
Red, white (or in this case, cream), and blue: a color combination to stir the heart and lift the spirits. Color-coordinated details—the period-style dolls' house and red chair, with its patriotic cushion, and the blue storage chest and side table—complete the look.

matching tones: butterflies at the crossroads

Finished size:
approx. 77" x 77"

Block size: 9" square

Number of blocks: 25

You will need:

FOR THE BUTTERFLY BLOCKS:
- 9 fat quarters (see page 11) for the background
- 7 fat quarters for butterflies and crossroads

TO COMPLETE THE QUILT:
- 4 yds. red fabric for sashing and borders
- 4¾ yds. fabric for backing
- 4¾ yds. 2-oz. fabric for batting
- ½ yd. blue fabric to make binding
- Matching sewing and quilting threads
All fabrics should be 44" wide.

RIGHT: SYMMETRY
In a quilt like this one, which consists of repetitions of the same basic block pattern, make sure that all the sashing strips are the same width so that the rows align.

1 For each block, cut four 2 ½" squares and four 2 ⅞" squares from each fabric. Cut the four 2 ⅞" squares in half diagonally to make eight triangles. Taking a ¼" seam, re-piece the triangles in pairs along the cut edge to make eight two-tone patches.

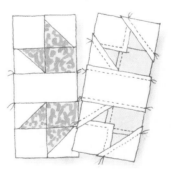
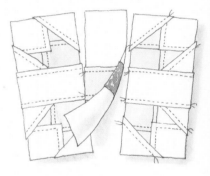

2 Lay out the patches as shown above. Taking a ¼" seam allowance, stitch the patches together in pairs, and then stitch two pairs together so that you have four large squares.

3 Cut four strips measuring 4½" x 1½" from light-colored fabric. Taking a ¼" seam allowance, stitch one strip between each vertical pair of four-unit patches. Press the seam toward the strips.

4 Cut a 1½" square from the dark fabric and, taking ¼" seams, stitch it between the two remaining strips to form a long strip. Right sides together, taking care to match seams, pin and stitch it to the rectangular units that you completed in Step 3.

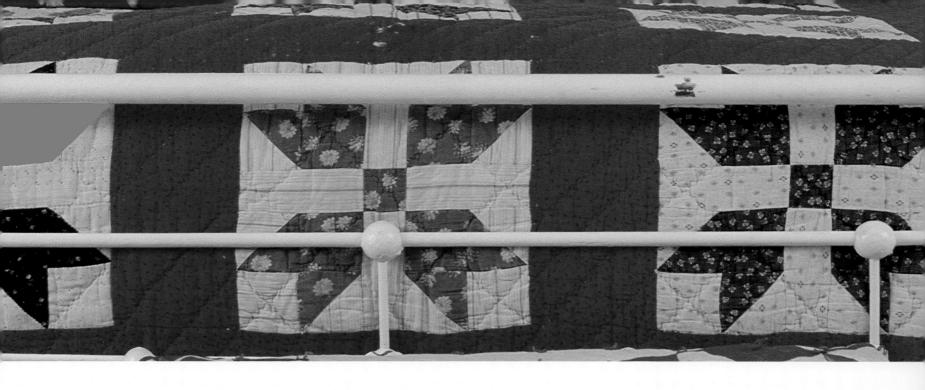

5 Make 25 blocks and lay them out in your chosen order, in five rows of five. Cut sashing strips 4½" x 9½" wide from the red background fabric. Machine stitch one strip to the right-hand edge of each block except those in the last vertical row. Machine stitch the sashed blocks together into horizontal strips. Measure the width of the horizontal rows and cut four 4½" strips to this length. Attach one of these strips below every horizontal row except the last one.

6 For the outer border, cut two strips the width of the quilt and 8½" wide and stitch to the top and bottom of the quilt. Then cut two strips the length of the quilt (including the borders already attached) and 8½" wide, and stitch these to the sides.

7 Assemble the quilt layers, pin, and baste. Mark and quilt a simple grid pattern on the quilt top.

8 To complete the quilt, add a single binding in a contrasting color (see page 148).

muted color: cotton reel

Many quilt patterns derive their name from domestic items—testimony to the lives of the women who first made them. This cotton reel pattern is created by placing light fabrics opposite light and dark opposite dark. The color placement, seemingly random, is in fact carefully done so that the few red patches are distributed evenly. Red is a warm color: your eye is drawn to it, and too much red in one section would destroy the visual balance of the quilt.

BELOW: SOFT SHADES
The soft colors used in this quilt—creams mixed predominantly with muted blues, browns, and occasional reds—give it a kind of faded charm that works particularly well in a country-style setting.

You will need:

● 15–16 fat quarters (see page 11) in ginghams, plaids, or other small-checked fabrics in muted colors

● 3¾ yds. cream fabric

● 4¾ yds. fabric for backing

● 4¾ yds. 2-oz. batting

● Matching sewing and quilting threads

All fabrics should be 44" wide.

Finished size:
approx. 80" x 72"

Block size: 4" square

Number of blocks: 360

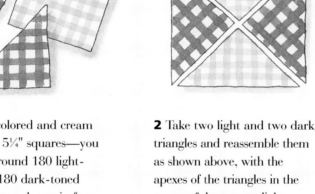

1 Cut the colored and cream fabrics into 5¼" squares—you will need around 180 light-toned and 180 dark-toned squares. Cut each one in four along the diagonal.

2 Take two light and two dark triangles and reassemble them as shown above, with the apexes of the triangles in the center of the square, light patches opposite light, and dark opposite dark. Taking a ¼" seam allowance, stitch two adjacent triangles to each other to form a larger triangle. Repeat with the other two triangles.

3 Stitch the two large triangles together to form a square, taking care to match the points precisely in the center. Make 360 blocks.

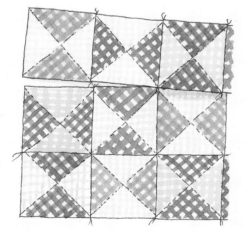

4 Lay out the blocks and, taking a ¼" seam, piece them in pairs. Piece each pair with the pair on the row below to make squares, and then piece the squares into larger squares, until you have completed the quilt top. You will need 18 rows of 20 blocks.

5 Assemble the quilt layers, pin, and baste. Outline quilt each triangle of each block with one line of stitching (see page 147). Make a fold-finish around the outside edge (see page 148).

plaid and tan checkerboard quilt

Put together a cozy winter quilt made from a warm chestnut brown and a vibrant red-and-black plaid; the colors harmonize beautifully. Why not make a smaller version to wrap around yourself as you curl up in your favorite armchair? Nothing could be easier to piece. To make it into a throw for a sofa or armchair, just leave out the batting.

RIGHT: WINTER WARMTH
The rich, warm colors of this quilt look fabulous against neutral white bed linen, with the chestnut-brown fabric providing a visual link with the polished wooden floor and door.

You will need:

- 3½ yds. chestnut-brown fabric
- 3½ yds. plaid fabric
- 7¾ yds. of 2-oz. batting
- 7¾ yds. fabric for backing
- ¾ yd. fabric to make binding
- Matching sewing and quilting threads

All fabrics should be 44" wide.

Finished size:
approx. 85" x 85"

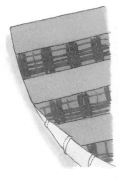   

1 Cut the tan and the plaid fabrics into strips 5½" wide. Taking a ¼" seam allowance, piece 17 strips together, alternating the fabrics and stitching the seams in opposite directions. Press each seam toward the darker fabric.

2 Cut the pieced fabric into strips 5½" wide and turn every alternate strip upside down. You will need 17 rows of 17 squares. Press the seams.

3 Taking a ¼" seam allowance, stitch the strips together to form the quilt top. Press the seams.

4 Assemble the quilt layers, pin, and baste.

5 Quilt with a grid pattern of diagonal lines. Finish by adding a single binding in plain fabric (see page 143).

multicolor maple-leaf wall hanging

This maple-leaf wall hanging is an exuberant and playful exercise in color, with fuchsia pink, turquoise, orange, bright green, and even a red-and-black plaid all vying for attention. Although each block is different, the pink and blue sashing helps to unify the piece by picking up on two colors that appear (in various tones) throughout the quilt.

Finished size:
approx. 68" x 68"
Block size: 12" square
Number of blocks: 25

For each block you will need:

- Twenty-five 15" squares of different colored fabrics for leaves
- Twenty-five 12" squares of different colored fabrics for backgrounds

TO MAKE UP THE QUILT:

- 1¼ yds. fabric for sashing
- 1 fat quarter (see page 11) in a contrasting color for the corner squares
- 4¾ yds. for backing and hanging sleeve
- 4¼ yds. of batting (optional)
- Matching sewing and quilting threads

All fabrics should be 44" wide.

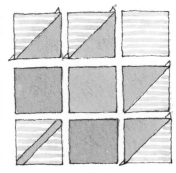

1 For each block, cut two squares measuring 4⅞" from both the leaf and the background fabrics, cut each one in half along the diagonal, and stitch four pieced triangle patches. Cut two 4½" squares from the background fabric and three from the leaf fabric.

2 For each block, make the "stem" by cutting a 6½" x 1½" strip from the leaf fabric. Fold under the raw edges by ¼" on each side and press. Topstitch it to one background square across the diagonal, stitching along both sides so that it lies flat, and trim off any excess.

3 Arrange the patches as shown, then stitch them together in three horizontal rows. Join the rows to make a block. Make 25 blocks and lay them out in five rows of five blocks each.

4 Taking a ¼" seam, stitch one length of 12½" x 4½" strip of sashing fabric (see page 11) underneath each block except for the blocks on the bottom row. Press the seams toward the border.

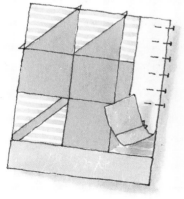

5 Then make the vertical sashing strips. Take one 12½" x 4½" strip of sashing fabric and one 2½" square in a contrasting color, and stitch them together, again with a ¼" seam. Make 16 of these strips and stitch one to the right-hand side of every block

except those in the last vertical row, taking care to match the seams. Press the seams toward the border.

6 Complete the top by stitching the blocks together in pairs or in threes. Assemble the quilt layers, pin, and baste. Quilt in the ditch to hold the layers together (see page 147), and self-bind (see page 148). Make a hanging sleeve (see page 135).

ABOVE: PATTERNS VS. SOLID COLORS
For maximum effect when making this design, use either two solid fabrics or one solid and one patterned fabric in each block. If both fabrics are patterned (as in the third block on the left side), the design will not stand out clearly.

LEFT: JAZZY PRIMARIES
This sunny bedroom, with its
brightly painted walls and
door and folk-style art, is
a veritable kaleidoscope of
color. The cool blues in the
quilt and painted chair help
to balance what might
otherwise be an over-
powering expanse of yellow.

jewel-bright mosaic quilt

This brightly colored design, in which tiny jewel-like squares of color
surround oases of calming blue, is perfect for a child's bedroom. A
smaller version would look fabulous as a cushion on a neutral sofa or
chair. The backing fabric is a cheerful, sunshine-yellow fabric, chosen
to match the color of the walls.

Although this looks like a very intricate and complex design, it
actually consists of straightforward double nine-patches interspersed
with blocks containing a large square set on point. Because the
mosaic-style squares are very small, this pattern offers a great way of
using up remnants of fabric left over from other projects.

Think carefully about your choice of colors. Experiment by moving
colors around to see how they look before you start piecing. If any
color clashes with another, reject it.

The mosaic squares are put together by stitching together three
strips of fabric in different colors and then cutting the strips vertically
to give strips of three identically-sized squares. You could piece them
individually by hand if you wish, but as each finished square measures
only 2 inches, you'd need the patience of a saint and the eyesight of
an eagle! The method shown here is far easier and quicker.

jewel-bright mosaic quilt

Finished size:
approx. 60" x 84"
Block size: 12" square

Number of blocks:
Block 1 – 18
Block 2 – 17

You will need:

● 19 to 20 fat quarters (see page 11) in colors of your choice
● 1½ yds. pale blue fabric
● 5 yds. of backing fabric
● 5 yds. of 2-oz. batting
● ¾ yd. to make binding in the color of your choice

All fabrics should be 44" wide.

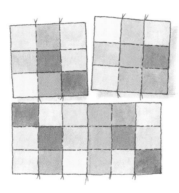

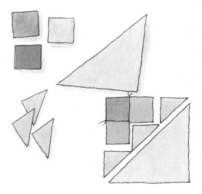

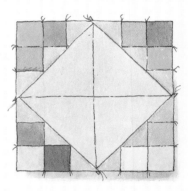

1 To make Block 1, take three strips of fabric in different colors—say, pale blue, yellow, and deep blue— 2½" wide and machine stitch them together taking a ¼" seam. Repeat with different colors to make a number of multi-colored pieces (the color arrangement is completely random in this quilt). Press the seams to one side. Cut each strip vertically into pieces that are 2½" wide.

2 Take three strips, turn them around so that you get completely random arrangements of color, and assemble them into a square, taking a ¼" seam allowance. Press. Stitch four of these 9-patch blocks together to make Block 1. Make 18 of these blocks in total.

3 To make Block 2, cut a 6⅞" square from pale blue fabric and cut it in half diagonally. Cut two 2⅞" squares in colors of your choice and cut them in half diagonally. Cut three 2½" squares in colors of your choice. Piece all the components as shown above to give a square unit.

4 Stitch four of these units together to make Block 2, as shown above. Make 17 blocks in total.

5 Starting with a Block 1 and alternating blocks, stitch five blocks together to make the first horizontal row. On the next row, start with a Block 2. Continue until you have made all the horizontal rows, and then stitch all the horizontal rows together to complete the quilt top.

RIGHT: BALANCED QUILTING
A decorative quilting motif
would be lost on the busy
mosaic-style blocks, and so a
simple grid pattern over these
areas suffices. The pretty
heart-shaped motifs add
texture and visual interest to
the large solid-blue squares.

6 Assemble the quilt layers,
pin, and baste. Quilt four
adjoining heart-shaped motifs
in the center of each pale blue
square and quilt the rest of the
quilt with a simple grid. Finish
by adding a single border in a
contrasting color (see page 148).

CHAPTER TWO

pattern

There are hundreds of recognized patchwork patterns and more are being devised all the time as quiltmakers explore new avenues and ideas. Different patterns often emerge when the same block is set in other ways.

From a craft that began as a thrifty way of using up leftover fabric or recycling worn clothes and bedcovers, patchwork has developed into an art form in its own right. Along the way wonderfully descriptive pattern names like Drunkard's Path and Hole in the Barn Door have evolved. Some pattern names reflect domestic life—Broken Dishes, Cotton Reel, and Baby Blocks. Others evoke the natural world—Flying Geese, Bear's Paw, and the many star patterns. Even political figures had patchwork patterns named for them—the pattern, Mr. Roosevelt's Necktie, for example, first appeared in *Practical Needlework* magazine around 1910. Of course, we'll never know who first came up with these patterns. We can only speculate on what their lives must have been like and what inspired them, but we owe them a deep debt of gratitude for they've left us with a rich legacy.

Originally, the designs would have been passed down from mother to daughter and shared with neighbors and friends. Itinerant peddlers hawking fabrics, pins and needles, and other essentials from settlement to settlement probably also played their part. From around the middle of the nineteenth century in America, however, patchwork patterns began to find their way into print in periodicals and magazines such as *Godey's Lady's Book* and *Peterson's*, and many of the pattern names we use today date from this period. A little later still, commercial quilt patterns became available: One very influential company was the Ladies' Art Company, founded by a German immigrant family. The fact that their catalogs in the 1890s contained some 300 patterns is surely proof of the huge appetite that existed for designs old and new.

LEFT: BARN RAISING
It's easy to see how some patterns got their names. This is one of many settings of the popular Log Cabin design.

RIGHT: OHIO STAR
A simple but very graphic pattern, Ohio Star is one of many star designs. It works very well in just two colors.

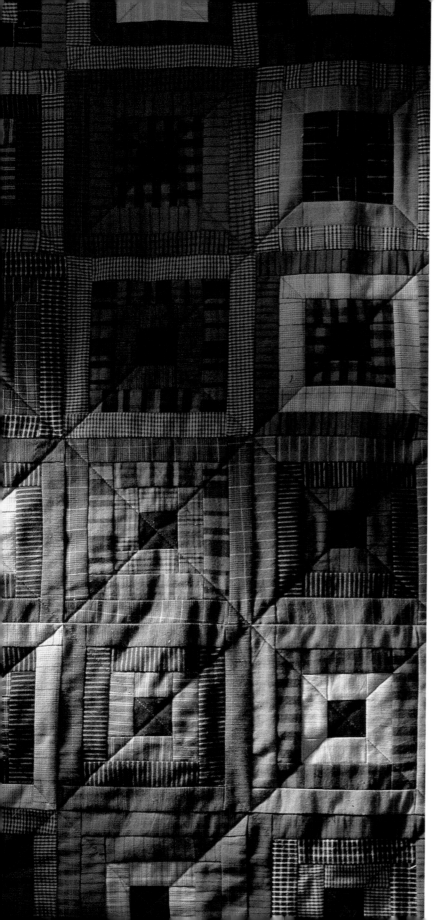

Quilting tradition: log cabin

The Log Cabin quilt has come to symbolize the pioneer spirit of America, and the names of many variations—Barn Raising, Sunshine and Shadow, Straight Furrow, Streak of Lightning—conjure up a harsh, but honest, frontier existence where people lived off the land and helped their neighbors. Even the Pineapple, which sounds far too exotic to be part of everyday life for the early settlers, is a traditional symbol of hospitality and it was a popular pattern for that reason.

No one knows for sure how the pattern originated, but it was well known during the Civil War; given Abraham Lincoln's "log cabin" campaign of 1860, some historians think it may have begun as a representation of the Union, though this has not been proven. By the 1870s, county fairs were offering prizes for Log Cabin quilts and the pattern's appeal has continued ever since.

Log Cabin allows you to create complex patterns from tiny scraps by altering the positioning of light and dark fabrics. Almost all Log Cabin variations are made up of blocks that consist half of light-colored strips and half of dark; it is the way the blocks are combined that creates the pattern (see page 67).

Nowadays, Log Cabin is usually strip pieced, but in the early days it was made using a technique known as foundation piecing, in which the fabric scraps were stitched to a foundation fabric. Because a foundation-pieced quilt top consists of two layers and the backing provides a third layer, very often such a quilt does not need any batting. Old Log Cabin quilts are often "tied" (see page 11) to hold the layers together rather than quilted.

LEFT: QUILT WITH A MESSAGE
This modern quilt harks back to the Civil War and the Underground Railroad: it is said that Log Cabin quilts with a black center were hung on laundry lines to indicate a safe haven for slaves fleeing to the north of the country.

RIGHT: COURTHOUSE STEPS
Each block captures the symmetry of a colonial-style building with a flight of steps leading up to the main entrance.

BELOW: STRAIGHT FURROW
One of a number of designs whose name evokes a rural, farming setting.

pattern names

It's a little disconcerting to discover that the same pattern can go by a number of different names. For example, the pattern known as LeMoyne Star is exactly the same as Lemon Star (the name became corrupted as the design traveled north), while Double Wedding Ring—probably one of the most popular patterns of all time—is also sometimes intriguingly referred to as Pickle Dish.

Patterns also changed their names over time. The pattern published by *Godey's Lady's Book* in 1835 as Honeycomb is now much more widely known as Grandmother's Flower Garden (see pages 122–125).

Sometimes quite small differences in the piecing can turn one pattern into another. In the nine-patch Churn Dash pattern, for example, the central square is the same size as the corner squares; when the central square is twice the size of the corner squares, then the pattern is known as Hole in the Barn Door. And although you'd never think so from the names, a Bear's Paw bears more than a passing resemblance to Turkey Tracks—both are pieced from similar configurations of squares and half-square triangles.

settings

One of the most fascinating things about patchwork is the way in which different patterns and visual effects emerge depending on how blocks are combined together. This is known as the setting, and there are several options that you can experiment with.

RIGHT: APPLIQUÉ QUILT
Red and green are a classic color combination that works well with all sorts of different patterns. The shapes of the appliqué design are very bold and cry out to be displayed against a plain backdrop.

The simplest option is to stitch together a number of identical blocks, with or without sashing, to make a repeating pattern. The Multicolor Maple-Leaf quilt on pages 50–51 is an example of this, as is the Stars upon Stars quilt on pages 92–95. This is really your only option for most representational blocks, as the pattern does not stand out as clearly when the blocks are pieced side by side.

With many other designs, however, secondary patterns emerge when you combine several blocks together and the way that you combine them (the "setting") can dramatically alter the final result.

You might choose to make all the blocks in the same colors and set them side by side. Or you could transpose the color values in half the blocks. In the Robbing Peter to Pay Paul quilt on pages 32–35 this approach has created a very fluid, flowing pattern. If all the main pieces had been in red, rather than half in red and half in white, the result would have been a very stark, geometric quilt—equally attractive but with a very different mood. The drawbacks of setting blocks side by side is that piecing needs to be very accurate and you may need a large number of blocks to reach the required quilt size.

RIGHT: PROFUSION OF PATTERNS
The patterns of the quilts in this charming bedroom range from the formality of the white-on-blue Album Patch to the colorful but apparently random piecing of the Crazy Quilt wall hanging. Also on the bed is a superbly stitched trapunto and corded quilt (see page 11) which dates from around 1830.

LEFT: ALBUM PATCH
This red-and-white version of the same pattern makes a dramatic tablecloth for any kitchen or dining room.

Changing the orientation of the blocks is another way to alter the look. Many Log Cabin designs, for example, have each block pieced in the same way from the same fabrics, but turning the squares through 90 or 180 degrees gives a different overall pattern. Among the best-known settings are Straight Furrow, which has diagonal lines across the quilt; Barn Raising, which forms concentric diamonds; Streak of Lightning—a dynamic zig-zag pattern; and Light and Dark, created by arranging blocks with four darks side by side.

"... patchwork is a good means of saving. It is naturally a crazy waste of time to tear cloth to pieces in order to arrange it anew into fantastic patterns; but ... a few shillings may be saved through the use of curtain and clothing scraps."

The American Frugal Housewife, Lydia Maria Child (31st ed., 1845)

You might choose to break up the pattern by alternating pieced blocks with squares in a solid color or by surrounding each block with strips of fabric that act as a kind of frame (this is known as sashing). The solid squares and sashing can either be in a color used in the block or a color that contrasts or tones with the block; again, the mood will vary depending on which option you select. Solid squares or sashing are often good choices with very busy patterns made up of lots of small pieces, as the solid colors provide both a visual resting place and an area that you can embellish with quilting. Quilts that are set as alternating pieced and solid blocks are quicker to make than quilts in which the blocks are set side by side, as every second block is a large square in a single color.

Finally, you can set the blocks "on point" in a diamond formation, setting the blocks side by side or interspersed with setting squares or sashing as above. Experiment with your favorite designs to see how many variations of setting you can come up with.

LEFT: INTRICATE PIECING
Mariner's Compass is among the most intricate of all patchwork patterns. This quilt is a superb example, in terms of its execution and its use of subtle fabrics in similar tones.

BELOW: CONTROLLED USE OF COLOR
A slightly simpler version of Mariner's Compass than the quilt shown opposite, but equally effective. Note the clever use of solid colors and small-patterned prints: no one element dominates and the result is a crisp, clean design.

Quilting tradition: double wedding ring

Double Wedding Ring quilts have long been popular as a way of commemorating a wedding or anniversary. The curved pieces appear to interlock and overlap and are said to symbolize the ever-changing state of married life.

Although the design dates back to the late nineteenth century, it seems to have reached its height of popularity in the 1920s and 1930s. The fact that it is traditionally pieced largely from scraps may account, at least in part, for this: a great number of Double Wedding Ring quilts (along with other scrapbag patterns, such as Dresden Plate) were made in the 1930s, during the Great Depression, when thrifty and desperate housewives had to recycle and "make do and mend" as never before. Many Depression-era Double Wedding Ring quilts were even made from old feedsacks, which at this time were often printed with patterns so that customers could reuse them, and these quilts are now highly collectible.

Because of its curved seams, Double Wedding Ring is not the easiest of designs to piece, and you need to take care when selecting the scraps for the rings. The fabric must be bold enough to make a statement, because the rings are the focal point of the design, but not overpowering. Double Wedding Ring quilts are usually made with a solid background fabric in pale colors, which allows the rings to stand out and also gives you the chance to indulge in some virtuoso quilting. However, light rings on a dark background can give equally dramatic results, as you can see from the quilt shown on the left.

LEFT: PATRIOTIC COLORS
Not quite Stars and Stripes, but the overall impact is just as impressive. The stars are appliquéd to the center of each block.

ABOVE LEFT: PRETTY PASTELS
Here the colors have been deliberately chosen to create an eye-catching pink-and-yellow color scheme. Not all Double Wedding Rings are pieced from scraps.

ABOVE RIGHT: PATTERNED PRINTS
A true scrapbag Double Wedding Ring quilt. A bias binding on the curved edges is the only border that is needed.

RIGHT: CLASSIC BLUE AND WHITE
Alternating horizontal and vertical stripes form the rings, with bold blue squares at the edge of each curve providing punctuation points within the design.

"... As I sift through a wooden box of old nightgowns, curtains, and dresses, I am looking for just the right materials, like words, to stitch together ..."

"Making It", Phyllis Theroux, *House Beautiful*, May 1999

double wedding ring

This pattern is considered by many people to be the highpoint of the quiltmaker's art, and it requires skill and confidence in piecing. Like Tumbling Blocks (see pages 76–77), it creates a kind of optical illusion: sinuous curves weave their way across the quilt top in a series of interlocking and overlapping rings like a three-dimensional puzzle.

The quilt shown here is a particularly fine example. Although at first glance it might look as if the rings have been appliquéd to the white background fabric, the background actually forms part of the patchwork pattern.

The rings themselves are pieced from scraps. The skill, of course, is in choosing fabric scraps that work well together. Because the pieces are very small, stick to tiny prints or solid colors, and avoid color clashes and strong contrasts. A lot of the printed fabrics used in this quilt include white, and this also helps to tie the whole quilt together because it links the rings with the background color.

Many Double Wedding Ring quilts have curved edges with a simple bias binding. Here, half blocks have been added to the sides to create straight edges.

LEFT: SOFT AND SUBTLE
Most of the prints in this quilt are light or middle tones in solids or very small patterns. Although no one color predominates, the overall effect is one of harmony.

double wedding ring

Finished size:
approx. 72" x 90"

Block size: 18" square

Number of blocks: 12

You will need:

FOR THE BLOCKS:
- 14 to 15 fat quarters in different patterns
- 3½ yds. white fabric for background pieces

All fabric should be 44" wide.

TO COMPLETE THE QUILT:
- 2 yds. white fabric for border
- ¾ yd. print fabric for border
- 5½ yds. fabric for backing
- 5½ yds. of 2-oz. batting
- Matching sewing and quilting threads

1 Using the pattern on page 152, make templates for background pieces A and B, adding a ¼" seam allowance all around. Cut eight A and four B pieces from the background fabric. Trace template C (the curved ring), again adding a ¼" seam allowance all around, and make eight full-size photocopies.

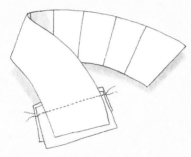

2 Cut strips of fabric big enough to cover the individual sections of the ring, including a ¼" seam allowance. Place your photocopy of template C on a flat surface, drawn side down. Take your first piece of fabric, center it right-side up over the first segment on the photocopy, and pin it in position.

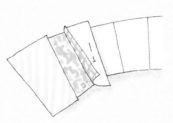

3 Right-sides together, pin your second strip of fabric over the first. Turn the piece over so that the photocopy is on top. Starting in the seam allowance, carefully stitch along and slightly beyond the marked stitching line.

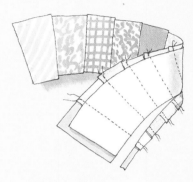

4 Turn the piece over so that the fabric is on top and trim the seam allowance to ¼". Turn back the second piece of fabric and press flat. Pin in place. Continue adding strips in this way until the photocopy is covered in fabric. Press and trim the pieced fabric curve and the photocopy underneath to the marked seam allowance. Make another seven curved units in the same way.

RIGHT: FLOWING CURVES
This close-up detail shows the
skill needed to piece the
curves so that the rings align
from one block to the next.

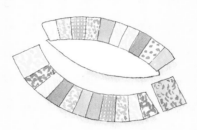

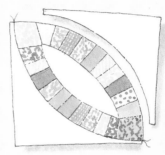

5 Take one curved unit and
one background piece B. Right
sides together, carefully match
the center and the ends and
pin together. Sew along the
sewing line, gently easing the
fullness of the curve as you go
so that the fabric doesn't
wrinkle. Make four units in
this way.

6 Take the remaining four
curved units that you completed
in Step 4 and, using template D,
add a square of fabric to each
end of each one. Stitch one of
these curves to each of the units
completed in Step 5, so that
you have four elliptical units.

7 Take two A background
pieces, and stitch one to each
side of one elliptical unit.

8 Make four more units like
this, assemble them as shown
left and stitch together to
form a block. Make 12 blocks
in total.

9 Next, stitch the blocks
together to make four rows
of three.

10 Cut a strip of white
background fabric 3½" wide
and construct the first border,
taking a ¼" seam. Repeat
with a 2½"-wide strip in a
contrasting fabric and finally
a 4½" strip in the white
background fabric.

11 For the quilting pattern,
mark a loose daisy shape in
the center of each block,
concentric oval shapes around
the border, and outline quilting
for the inner pieces of the
rings. Assemble the quilt layers,
pin, and baste. Quilt, following
your marked patterns, and
fold-finish (see page 148).

nine-patch

This is one of the simplest of all patchwork patterns. Square blocks, each one made up of nine smaller squares, are separated by strips of striped sashing material and solid squares in a contrasting color.

You can use the same fabrics for each block if you prefer, but varying the fabrics creates visual interest and is also a great way of using up small pieces of fabric left over from other projects.

You will need:

FOR THE BLOCKS:
2½ yds. dark fabric
3 yds. light fabric

TO COMPLETE THE QUILT:
- 3½ yds. striped fabric for sashing and border
- 1 yd. yellow fabric for corner squares on sashing
- 7¾ yds. of fabric for backing
- 7¾ yds. of 2-oz. batting
- Matching sewing and quilting thread

All fabrics should be 44" wide.

Finished size:
approx. 87" x 111"
Block size: 9" square
Number of blocks: 63

  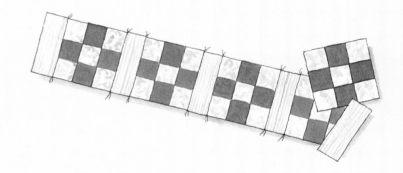

1 For each block, cut nine 3½" squares—five in light fabric and four from darker fabric. Taking a ¼" seam, stitch the squares together in the following sequence, to give three rows of three squares each: ABA, BAB, ABA. Press the seams to one side.

2 Stitch the three rows together to form a block, matching seams carefully as you work. Press the seams to one side. Make 63 blocks.

3 Lay out the blocks on a large, flat surface in nine rows of seven blocks each. Cut 142 sashing strips from striped fabric measuring 9½" x 3½" and eighty 3½" squares.

4 Sash each horizontal row of the quilt with the stripes of the sashing fabric running vertically.

RIGHT: INTRICATE PIECING
Setting nine-patch blocks with sashing gives a quilt a more formal feel than setting the blocks edge to edge. The dark, solid patches in each block help to anchor the design and balance the predominantly pastel prints. Delicate drapes and bed hangings complement the soft, feminine colors.

5 Next, make up the intermediate sashing rows. Here the stripes of the sashing fabric run horizontally. Starting and ending each row with a square and alternating squares and sashing strips, piece together eight squares and seven strips to make a row that runs the whole width of the quilt. Make 10 rows like this.

6 Stitch a row of sashing to the bottom of each row of nine-patches. Stitch the rows together, taking care to match the seams.

7 Mark a simple grid over the whole of the top. Assemble the quilt layers, pin, and baste. Machine stitch quilt.

8 Trim the top and batting to the same size. Trim the backing so that it is 1" bigger all around. Self-bind by folding the backing over to the top with a ½" turning.

tumbling blocks

Tumbling Blocks (also known as Baby Blocks) is one of a number of patterns that create a three-dimensional effect. You can vary the colors in different blocks if you wish, but the key is remembering to keep the color values (light, medium, and dark) in the same place in every block. A small-scale version of this design would look fabulous as a crib quilt in pastel shades or bright, primary colors.

Finished size: approx.
48" x 49"

Number of blocks: 137

You will need:

- 1 yd. fabric in a light color
- 1 yd. fabric in a medium color plus ½ yd. for filling-in pieces
- 1 yd. fabric in a dark color
- ½–¾ yd. for border
- 3 yds. of 2-oz. batting

- 3 yds. of backing
- ½ yd. fabric to make binding
- 2¼ yds. of fabric for frill (optional)
- Matching sewing and quilting threads

Fabrics should be 44" wide.

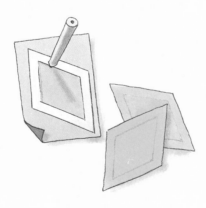

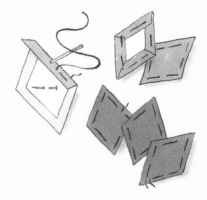

1 Trace patterns A, B, and C on page 153 and make window templates from template plastic. Follow the instructions for making templates on page 138.

2 Place the window template on the fabric, aligning the grain, and draw around the outer and inner lines. Cut out the fabric, cutting around the outer line.

3 Pin a paper template to the wrong side of each fabric patch, matching it with the inner line. Fold the excess fabric over to the wrong side and baste.

4 Assemble the tumbling blocks by whipstitching one shape of each color together to make a unit, taking care not to stitch through the backing papers.

RIGHT: OPTICAL ILLUSION
Tumbling Blocks is one of the
best known of all optical
illusion quilt designs.

5 Combine the desired number
of units by whipstitching along
the edges (see step 4, page 76).

6 Continue until the throw is
the required size. You will find
that there are uneven edges.
Fill these in by adding single
pieces of the appropriate shape
and color, using the patterns of
page 153—B shapes along the
left and right edge, C shapes
along the top and bottom and
D shapes in the corners.

7 Remove the basting stitches
and backing papers. Assemble
the quilt layers, pin, and baste.
finally, quilt in the ditch (see
page 147).

8 Cut 2½" strips from the
main color and make a single
border (see page 148). Here
a frilled border has been used
for decorative effect, but a
straight border would work
equally well.

grandmother's fan

This delightful fan design in delicate pastel shades and pretty floral fabrics is the perfect choice for a very feminine bedroom. Although the fans vary in color, the background to each block is in the same baby blue fabric, and the yellow quarter-circle in the corner of each block also provides continuity.

Finished size:
approx. 60" x 90"
Block size: 6" square
Number of blocks: 150

You will need:

FOR THE BLOCKS:
- Scraps of two contrasting fabrics for fan blades: 3yds. light and 2yds. dark in total
- 1 yd. bright yellow fabric for corners
- 3½ yds. pale blue fabric for background
All fabrics should be 44" wide.

TO COMPLETE THE QUILT:
- 5½ yds. fabric for backing
- 5½ yds. of 2-oz. batting
- ½–¾ yd. fabric to make binding
- Matching sewing and quilting threads

1 Trace the patterns on page 154, make templates, and cut out all the pieces. For each block, you will need to cut three "fan blades" (pattern piece B) in fabric A and two in fabric B.

2 Place the first two blades of the fan right sides together and sew together along one straight edge. Press the seam toward the darker fabric. Complete the rest of the fan in the same way, alternating fabrics A and B. Pin the background piece (C) in place and stitch it to the long curved edge of the fan. Carefully add the small yellow corner piece (A), making sure you do not stretch the curve.

3 Make 150 blocks. Lay out 15 rows of 10 blocks each, positioning them as follows:

Row 1:
Block 1: Corner piece is in bottom right corner.
Block 2: Corner piece is in top right corner.
Block 3: Corner piece is in bottom right corner, and so on to the end of the row.

Row 2:
Block 1: Corner piece is in bottom left corner.
Block 2: Corner piece is in top left corner.
Block 3: Corner piece is in bottom left corner, and so on to the end of the row.

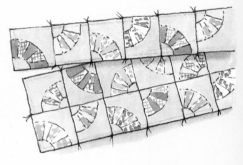

4 The pattern builds up, with the corners of diagonally adjacent blocks meeting to form two quarters of a circle. Stitch the blocks together to complete the quilt top.

RIGHT: FANFARE
Fan blocks are a common motif in quilts, but the way you position the blocks when you put the quilt top together alters the mood considerably. This design has a great sense of fluidity and movement.

5 On the plain background fabric, mark a daisy chain motif following the curve of the fan. Assemble the quilt layers, pin, and baste. Quilt the blades of the fans in the ditch (see page 147), the yellow flower centers in a simple grid pattern, and the plain background fabric following your earlier markings.

6 To finish, add a pink single binding (see page 148).

> ". . . when one of my grandchildren or great-
> grandchildren sees one o' these quilts, they'll
> think about Aunt Jane, and where I am then,
> I'll know I ain't forgotten . . ."
>
> *Aunt Jane of Kentucky*, Eliza Calvert Hall

barn raising

With its vibrant reds set opposite a crisp, clean white, this Barn Raising quilt is a surprisingly modern-looking interpretation of an old favorite.

Barn Raising, in which the blocks are arranged as concentric bands to make a diamond-shaped pattern, is just one of many variations on the traditional Log Cabin design. Like other Log Cabin patterns, it is worked by adding strips of fabric around a central square. The square is said to represent either the chimney or the hearth—the heart of the home—while the strips around it are the logs that make up the walls of the cabin.

When it comes to quilting, Log Cabin quilts require very little, if any, embellishment. The logs are generally so narrow that the effect of an elaborate quilting motif would simply be lost, and so a grid pattern, or quilting "in the ditch," is normally sufficient.

LEFT: DIAGONAL DYNAMISM
Rich, warm reds and browns against dark, polished wood—an elegant and welcoming combination.

barn raising

Finished size: 90" x 90"

Block size: 10" square

Number of blocks: 64

You will need:

FOR THE BLOCKS:

● ½ yd. red fabric for center squares

● Scraps 1½" wide in four dark fabrics totalling 4½ yds.

● Scraps 1½" wide in white fabric totalling 5 yds.

TO COMPLETE THE QUILT:

● 2 yds. white fabric

● 1¾ yds. assorted dark fabrics

● 8 yds. fabric for backing

● 8 yds. of 2-oz. batting

● Matching sewing and quilting threads

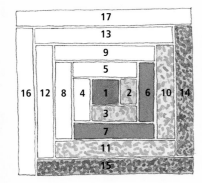

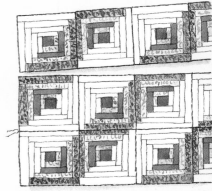

1 Cut 1½" strips in your chosen fabrics and one 2½" center square in red.

2 Taking a ¼" seam, stitch one dark strip to the center square, right sides together. Trim the strip to the same length as the square. Press the seam to one side.

3 Right-sides together, add the second dark strip. Again trim and press.

4 Add two light strips to complete the first round. Continue adding dark and light strips until you have completed four rounds and the block is complete. Make 64 blocks.

5 Lay out the blocks on a large, flat surface, arranging them to form concentric diamonds. (The illustration above shows the top left corner.) Stitch the blocks together to complete the quilt top.

6 Cut the white fabric into strips 1½" wide and the dark fabrics used for the blocks into strips 5" wide and stitch together in pairs, taking a ¼" seam. Cut each pieced strip vertically into 1½" strips and stitch pairs of strips together following the order of dark fabrics used in the blocks.

7 Rearrange the strips at an angle of 45° so that they form points, and machine stitch together to form a border.

8 Cut 3" strips of white fabric and attach to all sides of the quilt as a border. Attach the pieced border to the white border.

9 Assemble the quilt layers, pin, and baste. Quilt with a regular grid pattern (see pages 145–146). Self-bind to finish the quilt (see page 148).

ABOVE: COMPLEMENTARY QUILTING
A simple grid, running at right angles to the "logs," adds texture to the quilt without distracting from the pattern.

double Irish chain

No one knows exactly when or where the Irish Chain pattern originated. Despite the name, we can't even be sure that it came from Ireland—indeed, to add to the confusion, in Ireland itself the pattern is sometimes referred to as American Chain! But whatever its origins, the pattern has been popular with quilters since the early 1800s and may be one of the oldest block patterns.

"... The history of quilts is like its subject — a rich story sewn together from thousands of scraps of folklore and mythology ..."

Country Living's Country Quilts, (The Hearst Corporation, 1992)

All Irish Chain patterns, whether they're Single, Double, or Triple, are constructed by alternating two blocks. The first block is pieced, usually from just two colors. The second may be either pieced or a single piece of fabric, but it is made predominantly from one solid-color fabric. When the blocks are put together, a chain pattern appears which runs diagonally across the quilt.

The quilt shown here is an interesting variation on the norm: the blocks are set on point (see page 67), which results in the chain running up and down in a gridlike pattern. And instead of using just two colors in the first block, the quilter has constructed a multicolor mosaic which stands out dramatically against the plain cream background. The result is a stylish and elegant throw that combines the very best of old and new—a quilting tradition that goes back 200 years alongside a very contemporary feeling for color and design.

LEFT: GRAPHIC ELEGANCE
As in so many patchwork patterns, it is only when a number of blocks are combined that the real pattern of Double Irish Chain can be seen.

double Irish chain

Finished size: 77" x 77"

Block size: 10" square

Number of blocks:

Block 1 – 25

Block 2 – 16

You will need:

FOR THE BLOCKS:
- 11 fat quarters in varying colors
- 3 yds. fabric in cream color

TO COMPLETE THE QUILT:
- ¾ yd. fabric in cream for the border
- ¾ yd. blue fabric for the border

- 4¾ yds. fabric for backing
- 4¾ yds. of batting
- ½ yd. cream fabric for binding
- Matching sewing and quilting threads

All fabrics should be 44" wide.

1 To make Block 1, cut five colored fabric into strips 2½" wide. Taking a ¼" seam, machine stitch them together. Repeat with different colors to make a number of multicolored strips, making sure you have a white strip in the center of at least half the strips. Cut each strip vertically into pieces that are 2½" wide.

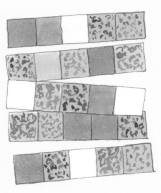

2 Take five strips, turn them around so that you get random arrangements of color, and lay them out in a square, making sure you have a white patch in the center of each outer edge. Taking a ¼" seam allowance, stitch the strips together to form a square. Make 25 blocks.

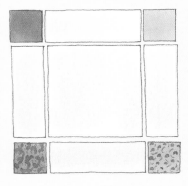

3 To make Block 2, cut a 6½" square from plain cream fabric, four strips measuring 6½" x 2½" in cream, and four colored 2½" squares for the corners. Assemble into a block. Make 16 blocks.

4 Lay out the blocks on point as shown above, alternating rows of blocks 1 and 2.

RIGHT: CHAIN ON POINT
It is hard to visualize how this gridlike chain will work until you have combined a number of blocks, but the effect is both stylish and dramatic.

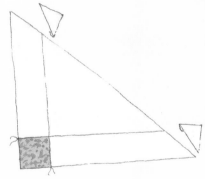

5 Cut one 6⅞" cream square and cut it in half along the diagonal, two cream strips measuring 8⅞" x 2½", and one colored 2½" square. Piece as shown above, then trim to make a triangle. Make 16 triangles. Cut a 7¼" cream square diagonally in quarters to make filling triangles for the four corners of the quilt top.

6 Lay out the blocks in rows as shown above.

7 Fill in the gaps around the edge of the quilt with the triangular pieces and corner triangles made in Step 5 and piece the rows together.

8 Make a blue and white sawtooth border, following the instructions on pages 40–41. Attach the border to the quilt. Fill in the corners with a solid blue square.

9 Assemble the quilt layers, pin, and baste. Quilt with a simple grid pattern or other pattern of your choice.

10 Finish with a single binding in cream (see page 148).

embroidered fan hanging

This stunning red and black quilt, which was probably made in the last quarter of the nineteenth century, combines two elements that were the very height of fashion at that time: oriental-style motifs, which became hugely popular after the 1876 Philadelphia Centennial Exposition at which more than 250 Japanese exhibitors showed their wares, and embroidered embellishments so beloved of the Victorians.

"... you see we used to sit under the pines and sew, and talk a great deal all the ladies ... and I liked it very much."

Eight Cousins, Lousia May Alcott

The fans are constructed using the "English" method of paper piecing (see page 142). Precise measuring and stitching are essential in order to get all the pieces to match.

Instead of keeping the fan in the same corner of the block every time, the quilter has cleverly created a wave-like pattern that runs through the whole quilt. Each block is embellished with chain and stem stitch embroidery. You can either copy the design shown here or choose your own motifs, but try to find examples with soft, flowing lines that will balance the geometric feel of the fans. The key is knowing when to stop: too much embroidery would detract from the very precise piecing of the fans, while too little would leave large expanses of unadorned fabric.

RIGHT: FREE AND EASY
Simple freestyle embroidery embellishes the blocks and allows the quilter plenty of scope for individuality.

embroidered fan hanging

Finished size:
approx. 78" x 78"

Block size: 12" square

Number of blocks: 36

You will need:

FOR THE BLOCKS:
- 3 yds. background fabric
- ½ yd. fabric for corners of fans
- 1¾ yds. fabric in each of two colors for fan blades
- Embroidery threads in the colors of your choice

TO COMPLETE THE QUILT:
- 1 yd. fabric for border
- 4¾ yds. fabric for backing
- 4¾ yds. of batting
- Matching sewing and quilting threads

1 Trace the pattern on page 155 onto stiff paper or thin card and cut out templates. Pin the templates to the fabric and cut out, allowing a ¼" seam allowance all around on each piece. Fold the surplus fabric over to the reverse side of the template and baste.

2 With right sides together, alternating red and black wedge shapes, overstitch the eight wedge pieces (marked B on the template) that form the main body of the fan.

3 To complete the fan shape, stitch the main body of the fan to the shape marked C on the template. Join the piece marked A on the template to the fan to complete the block. Make 36 blocks. Remove the backing papers.

4 Trace embroidery motifs of your choice onto tracing paper and make tiny pin pricks along all the lines of the design. Place the tracing paper right-side up on the fabric and run dressmaker's chalk along the pin-prick lines to transfer the pattern to the fabric.

5 Embroider over the lines of the motif in a decorative stitch—chain stitch is a good choice for winding, floral motifs. You can also stitch over the seam lines between each wedge of the fan. Join the blocks together in six rows of six so that the fans form a wave pattern across the quilt (see the photograph, opposite). Cut 3½" strips for the border and attach using the "top and tail" method (see page 143). Assemble the quilt layers, pin, and baste. Quilt in the ditch (see page 147). Complete by adding a single binding (see page 148).

RIGHT: BOLD AND BEAUTIFUL
Strong color contrasts are important in this design. Although you might want to change the colors to complement your own décor, it is hard to think of a combination more dynamic and eye-catching than the red and black shown here.

stars upon stars

Stars have long been a popular motif for quilters and this dramatic blue and white design, in which tiny stars seem to radiate outward from a central blue star, was published by the Ladies' Art Company around 1898. It is pieced entirely from diamonds using the English paper-piecing method—time-consuming to do, but it enables you to cut and match the sharp angles very precisely. Although it looks as if it is built up from concentric rows of diamonds, the first stage is to piece sixteen small diamonds together to make a large diamond; then piece eight of these large diamonds to make the whole star.

Blue and white are a classic color combination. Look closely, however, and you'll see that the blue fabric used here actually has tiny white spots on it. This gives it a luminous vibrancy that adds life to the design and seems particularly appropriate for a star pattern. Solid colors do sometimes deaden a design, so experiment with small prints to see what difference they make.

If you're daunted by the idea of piecing over 1,000 diamonds to make the whole quilt, why not make just a single block to use as a wall hanging? It would make a fabulous, eye-catching display on a plain white wall.

LEFT: STARBURST SPLENDOR
This is surely one of the most dramatic of all the many star patterns; it looks equally good as a multicolored design.

stars upon stars

Finished size:
approx. 90" x 90"

Block size: 22" square

Number of blocks: 9

You will need:

FOR THE STARS:

- 2½ yds. blue fabric
- 2½ yds. white fabric for diamonds plus 2½ yds. white fabric for filling-in pieces

TO COMPLETE THE QUILT:

- 1½ yds. white fabric
- 3 yds. blue fabric
- 8 yds. of backing fabric
- 8 yds. of 2-oz. batting
- Matching sewing and quilting threads

1 Using pattern A on page 156, make paper templates for the diamond and triangle shapes. For each block, cut 64 white diamonds and 64 blue ones (template A). Pin a backing paper to the wrong side of each diamond, matching the edges of the paper to the marked stitching line. Fold the seam allowance over the paper and baste.

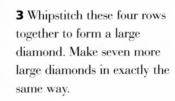

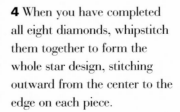

2 Take two white and two blue diamonds and, starting with a white one, whipstitch them together to form a row, alternating the colors. Repeat the process, this time starting the row with a blue diamond. Repeat these two rows once more to give four rows.

3 Whipstitch these four rows together to form a large diamond. Make seven more large diamonds in exactly the same way.

4 When you have completed all eight diamonds, whipstitch them together to form the whole star design, stitching outward from the center to the edge on each piece.

5 Using templates B and C on page 156, cut four white squares and four white triangles. Check that the templates match the gaps before cutting the material. Add the white corner squares, stitching outward to the edge of the square in each direction. To finish the block, add white filling-in triangles to the points, stitching outward from the points of the triangles.

RIGHT: POINTS GALORE
This close-up detail shows
the precision needed to
match all the points
accurately.

7 For the sashing between the
two rows, measure the length
of the quilt and cut eight blue
and four white 2½" strips to
this length. You will need to
join lengths of fabric to achieve
the correct length. Stitch the
strips together and stitch
them in place.

6 Arrange the blocks in three
rows of three. Cut twenty-four
22½" x 2½" strips of blue
spotted fabric and twelve 22½"
x 2½" white strips. Stitch them
together to make twelve bands
of blue, white, and blue. Attach
one to the top and one to the
bottom of the central block in
each row, stitch on the top and
bottom blocks in each row, and
attach a final blue, white, and
blue sashing strip to the top
and bottom of each row.

8 Assemble the quilt layers,
pin, and baste. Echo quilt the
individual diamonds in the star
blocks and the triangles (see
page 147), and quilt the corner
squares of the start blocks in a
diamond-shaped design. Self-
bind following the instructions
on page 148.

CHAPTER THREE

texture

There are two types of texture in quilting. First, there is the texture of the fabrics: cotton, velvets, silks, and even organzas can be incorporated. Second, there is the texture of the quilting: different quilting methods create different effects.

fabric texture

For any dedicated quilter or stitcher, the texture of a fabric is one of its main attractions: think of the thick pile of luxurious velvets, or the sleekness of raw silk, or the comforting softness of wool. Each has a very different texture and imparts a particular feel to a quilt.

Although many quilts are made from cotton, there is also a long tradition of using other fabrics. Often the type of fabric can help us to date antique quilts. During the Colonial period, for example, many wholecloth quilts were made of linsey-wolsey—a combination of linen and wool which, when backed with coarse woolen fabric, made a particularly warm quilt. Calimanco is a finer version of linsey-wolsey with a smooth finish. Following the invention of the cotton gin in 1793, cotton became much more readily available. And in the late nineteenth century, silks and velvets found their way into the richly decorated crazy quilts that were so popular at that time. It's generally easier to make a quilt all in the same weight and type of fabric, but mixing fabrics can create interesting texture and variety.

Even when you make a quilt entirely in one fabric, such as cotton, you can still exploit the visual differences between fabric patterns. A dark, solid color, for example, tends to look heavier than a light print; so bear this in mind as a useful way of creating textural contrasts in your work.

". . . little girls often have a great many small bits of cloth and large remnants of time . . . it is better for them to make cradle-quilts for their dolls, or their baby brothers, than to be standing around wishing they had something to do."

The Little Girl's Own Book, Lydia Maria Child (1832)

LEFT: TIED IN KNOTS
Ties create a rough-and-ready texture that is perfectly suited to rustic, country-style interiors.

BELOW: SOFT, GLOWING VELVET
This beautiful crazy patchwork throw is made from rich, heavy velvets that seem to glow in the firelight. On the chimney mantle hang two velvet Christmas stockings, one made using a Grandmother's Flower Garden motif (see pages 122–125).

tied quilting

The simplest and oldest method of quilting is to thread lengths of yarn through all three layers at regular intervals and knot them to secure them in place.

Tying is a great way to start quilting. It's very quick and easy to do, and you don't need to worry about your stitching skills (unlike conventional quilting, where the aim is to keep the stitches as small and even as possible to give a very regular finish). Tying has one very practical advantage, too: it allows you to undo the knots and remove the batting for cleaning.

The other major advantage of tying is that it gives you the opportunity to introduce wonderful textures into your quilts. The technique tends to give a much softer, more billowy texture than conventional running stitches. If you leave the ties showing on the top of the quilt, the materials you use can also create interesting textural contrasts: for example, chunky yarn in either a toning or a contrasting color will give a very rustic, homemade look, while shiny ribbons can look more sophisticated. And you can even attach embellishments such as buttons or bows to the ties for extra decoration and texture.

"At your quilting, maids don't dally,
Quilt quick if you would marry,
A maid who is quiltless at twenty-one
Never shall greet her bridal sun!"

Traditional poem

RIGHT: DECORATIVE TIES
The box cushion on this settle is pieced from alternating dark and light squares. Placing simple yarn ties on the joins maintains the geometry of the design and adds visual interest.

BELOW: COZY COLORS
Earthy shades of red, brown, and mustard give this tied quilt a lovely cozy feel that complements the Victorian-style room perfectly.

get the look: homespun rustic

The cushion is made of alternating light and dark squares of openweave cotton, tied with thick strands of cotton or yarn. You don't even need to worry about matching the seams precisely: a little irregularity adds to the homespun, informal feel.

Country-style furniture and fittings such as the distressed wooden furniture, battered lantern, and small cupboard with a punched-tin pattern on the doors can be bought inexpensively in junk shops and at garage sales.

Chunky earthenware bowls filled with fruit and informal arrangements of wild or dried flowers work well in this kind of interior.

Old prints and photographs, whether they're of famous individuals or family members, add to the period feel.

quilting stitches

Running stitch is probably the first stitch that many of us learn to make. Its original purpose in quilting was nothing more than to hold the layers of a quilt together, and it seems almost unbelievable that something so simple should be able to create so many different effects. But quilting stitches serve a decorative, as well as a functional, purpose: they give texture to the quilt and, when well executed, are a work of art in their own right. The best examples are stitched with such technical skill, consistency, and artistic flair that they almost take your breath away.

For beginners, the easiest way to start is to quilt "in the ditch." This just means stitching along or just beside the seam lines, and so no complicated marking is involved. The quilting stitches themselves will barely be visible, though their effect will certainly be seen. This method is particularly suitable for designs that consist of many small pieces, such as Log Cabin, as it creates texture without conflicting with the pattern.

Then there are outline and echo quilting. Outline quilting is a single line of stitching that follows the shape of a motif on the quilt top; it can be worked either inside or outside the motif. Echo quilting is a series of evenly spaced lines around a motif. Neither outline nor echo quilting need to be marked. Both these methods have the effect of throwing the motif into sharp relief and focusing attention on the shapes within the pattern.

LEFT: MIXING QUILTING PATTERNS
This wholecloth quilt shows three different types of quilting pattern: a simple filling pattern of a diamond grid on the quilt top, a decorative cable, and finally a floral motif around the scalloped edge.

OPPOSITE: QUILTING "IN THE DITCH"
Quilting along the seam lines, as here, is a good choice when you are using a printed fabric. It holds the quilt together, and provides a little texture, without detracting from the print pattern.

"Filling" designs, as the name implies, are generally used to cover large areas of a quilt. They can be used over the entire quilt or reserved for certain areas such as the background of blocks. They can consist of a simple pattern of diagonal lines or diagonal lines that cross each other at 90° to create a diamond pattern, or more complicated designs that need to be marked on the fabric, such as the interlocking semi-circles that make up a pattern known as Clamshell. The most important thing to remember with filling stitches is to be sure to keep the spacing even. The regularity of the stitching creates a very graphic-looking and highly textured quilt, even though the colors are actually very restrained.

There is also a huge range of nongeometric motifs such as flowers, feathers, hearts, and cables. When stitched on large areas of solid color, the effect can be truly spectacular. A wide range of quilting patterns is available commercially for you to trace onto your quilts.

For many people, the ultimate in quilting must be these elaborate quilting motifs. Whitework quilts, Amish quilts, and the nineteenth-century wholecloth quilts of Northeast England and Wales are all among the most dazzling displays of virtuoso needlecraft you could ever wish to see. Intricate motifs—hearts, wreaths, flowers, and feathers—are all picked out by means of tiny, evenly spaced running stitches and it was not unusual for there to be 18 to 20 stitches per inch.

Modern quilters should not feel discouraged by this, however! After all, in those days girls started sewing almost as soon as they were old enough to hold a needle—and so by the time they reached their

OPPOSITE: DIAMOND GRID
With their filling pattern of a simple diamond grid, these quilts rely entirely on texture, rather than color or pattern, for their impact.

ABOVE: MATCHING PILLOWS
A close-up detail of the matching pillows. Note that instead of extending the grid pattern right to the edge, the quilter has stitched two equally spaced lines around the center of the cushion to provide a kind of frame for the quilting pattern.

RIGHT: TEXTURED QUILTS, SMOOTH WALLS
With these smooth, pale walls and doors, it's essential to introduce a textural element such as the quilts to prevent the room from looking bland.

teenage years, they had probably had more practice than most of us will manage in a lifetime. Batting, too, was thinner and therefore easier to stitch than it is today.

Finally, there are also techniques such as corded quilting and trapunto, which are usually done in white thread on white fabric. Both of these methods involve padding the quilting motifs to create a raised, three-dimensional effect that can add interest to the piece without adding color.

Corded quilting is used for linear motifs and involves pulling a needle threaded with cotton yarn or cord through a stitched channel to create a delicate effect.

Trapunto is used for larger, nonlinear motifs such as flowers. In this method, a coarse backing fabric is basted to the quilt top and the quilting design is stitched through both layers; then small bits of cotton are pushed through the weave of the backing fabric to pad out the design (with very large motifs, it may be necessary to cut a slit in the backing fabric).

LEFT: WHOLECLOTH AND PATCHWORK TEXTURAL CONTRASTS
The texture of the white quilted bedspread contrasts well with the smoother, patchwork star quilt on top and helps to relieve the solid blue of the walls.

RIGHT: TEXTURE UPON TEXTURE
Here, too, texture is piled upon texture to great effect. The white trapunto quilt is topped by a patchwork coverlet of tiny mosaic-style squares quilted with a filling pattern of diamonds.

LEFT: BREAKING UP COLOR
WITH TEXTURE
These large expanses of
pastel colors would look
monotonous were it not
for the soft, flowing lines
of the quilting patterns.
Both the green and white
quilts are embellished
with a combination of
geometric shapes and
intricate curved patterns.

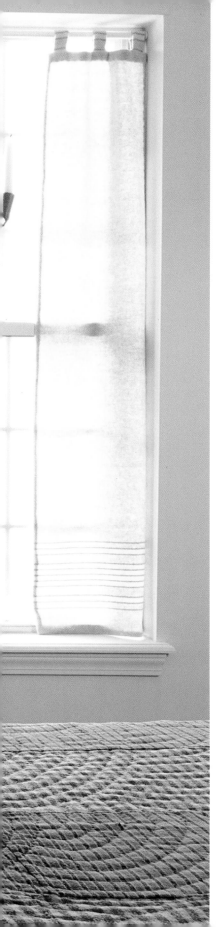

choosing quilting motifs

On a wholecloth quilt, where the actual quilting provides the main visual interest for the piece, you can opt for pretty much anything that strikes your fancy—a grid pattern for a bold, graphic effect; an intricate central medallion in the shape of a feathered wreath or star; flowing cables around the outer border. Vintage wholecloth quilts often have incredibly intricate motifs stitched into them, but simple designs can look equally effective. Choose something that will feel good as well as look good. You can really let your creativity guide you.

When you're doing the quilting for a pieced top, however, you also need to think about how the quilting motif complements the pattern, and how the piece will look as a whole. This can also be a wonderful opportunity to create your own individual style on a piece and make a popular pattern look unique. Try using curved motifs such as flowers or overlapping semi-circles to soften the effect of very linear patchwork patterns and provide a visual contrast, and cover large areas of solid color with filling patterns or large individual motifs for extra visual interest and texture.

LEFT: SOFTENING THE PATTERN
The curved lines of the quilting pattern soften the linear, checked fabric.

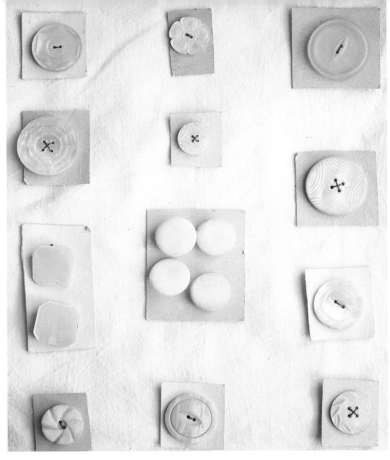

breaking the boundaries

Quilters have never been afraid to adapt patterns to suit their own tastes and requirements. Indeed, this is one of the things that makes it such a fascinating craft: color and fabric choice, pattern, and setting style are all at the discretion of the individual quilter, which means that each piece is unique. You could give the same basic block pattern to ten different quilters, and the chances are that they would come up with designs that look so different you would find it hard to believe they had the same starting point.

Contemporary quilters are branching out as never before, and one aspect of this is the use of unusual fabrics. Although 19th-century crazy quilts and show quilts broke new boundaries with their use of silks, velvets, and other luxurious fabrics, cotton has historically been the most commonly used fabric for quilts. Nowadays, however, anything goes! From delicate voiles and organzas placed over appliqué motifs to mute the colors as if they're being seen through mist to lurex and metallic fabrics that glint and sparkle, there are literally no limits.

Quilters are also incorporating techniques from other areas of needlecraft—and, indeed, from other craft disciplines altogether—in their work. Fabric dyeing, painting and stenciling, embroidery techniques: anything is grist to their mill. And finally, a whole range of embellishments, from buttons and bows to sequins and Indian shisha mirrors, are finding their way into quilts. If there is one phrase that sums up quilting today, it is surely individuality of expression.

There is no limit to what
you can use to embellish a
quilt. Color-coordinated
collections of buttons and
other trimmings such as
beads, sequins, and ribbons
also make great decorative
displays.

" She ushered her guests into the parlor, where the great quilting frame was stretched. It occupied nearly the entire room. There was just enough space for the quilters to file around and seat themselves four on a side".

A Quilting Bee in Our Village, Mary Eleanor Wilkins Freeman

tied eight-point star

Tying is a simple, yet very effective, way of holding the three layers of a quilt together. Instead of stitching patterns or motifs over the quilt, you simply make a series of knots at regular intervals, taking the yarn or thread through all three layers. Because you don't have to worry about making even stitches, as you would in normal quilting, tied quilts can be much thicker than normal.

You can make the ties on the reverse of the quilt if you want them to be unobtrusive, but making them on the quilt top and leaving long tails of yarn, as in this quilt, is a great way of adding texture and visual interest to the quilt.

Use embroidery thread or knitting yarn to make the ties, or even narrow ribbon—but check that whatever you use is colorfast. The choice of color is up to you: you can either select a color that blends with the fabrics used in the quilt top or one that contrasts. For extra decoration, you can even attach bows or stitch buttons over the ties.

As a decorative finish, tying is probably best suited to rough-and-ready, rustic style quilts.

LEFT: DECORATIVE YARN TIES
The rustic, homespun feel of the quilt is enhanced by decorative ties in a color that complements both the blocks and the background squares.

tied eight-point star

Finished size:
approx. 79" x 79"

Block size: 8" square

Number of blocks:
49 pieced + 36 plain squares
24 + 4 fill-in triangles

You will need:
FOR THE STAR BLOCKS:
- 2¼ yds. background fabric
- 2¼ yds. star fabric
- 3¼ yds. plain fabric
Fabric should be 44" wide.

TO COMPLETE THE QUILT:
- 4¾ yds. fabric for backing
- 4¾ yds. of 4-oz. batting
- Matching sewing and quilting threads
- Yarn for the ties in a dark color

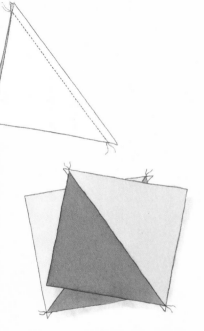

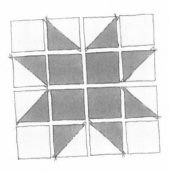

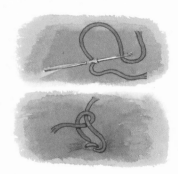

1 For each block, cut four 2⅞" squares from fabric A and four from fabric B. Cut them in half diagonally to give eight right triangles. Taking a ¼" seam allowance, stitch together one triangle A and one triangle B along the diagonal to give a two-tone square. Make seven more two-tone patches in the same way and press.

2 Cut four 2½" squares from each fabric. Arrange them with the two-tone patches in rows, as shown, then join them into four horizontal rows, each containing four squares. Stitch the four rows together to form a block. Make 49 blocks.

3 Cut thirty-six 8½" squares and twenty-four 8⅞" squares from the background fabric. Cut the larger squares in half along the diagonal. Lay out the blocks to make the quilt top on a large, flat surface.

4 Place the blocks on point, alternating pieced blocks and solid 8⅞" squares, using the triangles to fill in the gaps around the edges and make a straight edge.

5 Cut two 9¼" squares in half diagonally and position them at the corner. Taking a ¼" seam, assemble the quilt top.

6 Assemble the quilt layers, pin, and baste.

7 Take a darning needle and a double length of dark-colored yarn. Make a stitch through all layers where the tie will be, followed by a second stitch at the same place, and use a square knot to fasten the ends. Make a tie at every corner of every pieced block, halfway along every side of each pieced block, and in the center of every plain block.

8 Self-bind the quilt to finish (see page 148) by folding the backing to the front.

Amish nine-patch quilt

This quilt is a beautiful example of how simple quilting stitches can bring solid squares of color to life; a flowing, floral motif is worked in the center of each square, its curved shape counterbalancing the straight edges of the patchwork blocks. The use of large but simple geometric shapes, such as squares and rectangles, is typical of quilts made in the Amish tradition.

The colors are typically Amish and are combined with great skill, with rich blues contrasting with a deep, almost burgundy, red.

Note the block of pink and blue patches on the left of the photograph. This may be a "superstition block"—a common feature of Amish and many other quilts: because only God can create something perfect, deliberate mistakes (perhaps a patch or block in a different color from those used elsewhere in the quilt, or a motif turned upside down) are often incorporated into the design as a symbol of the quiltmaker's humility. The quantities given in the instructions overleaf assume that all the nine-patch blocks will be made from the same two colors, but you could vary the design by introducing blocks in another color combination if you wish.

RIGHT: SIMPLE SQUARES
Nine-patch blocks and solid squares alternate in this carefully controlled but vibrantly colored design. Fine hand quilting is a feature of Amish quilts, and stylized floral motifs such as the one used here are popular.

Amish nine-patch quilt

Finished size:
approx. 66" x 90"

Block size: 9" square

Number of nine-patch blocks: 35

Number of solid blocks: 24

You will need:

FOR THE NINE-PATCH BLOCKS:
● 2 yds. red fabric
● 1½ yds. mid-blue fabric

FOR THE SOLID BLOCKS:
● 2¾ yds. dark blue/indigo fabric

TO COMPLETE THE QUILT:
● 1 yd. red fabric for border
● 5 yds. dark blue/indigo fabric for backing
● 5 yds. of 2-oz. batting
● Matching sewing and quilting threads

All fabrics should be 44" wide.

1 For each nine-patch block, cut nine 4" squares—five in red and four in blue fabric. Starting with a red square in the first row and alternating the colors, stitch the squares together to give three rows of three squares each, taking ¼" seams. Press the seams to one side.

2 Stitch the three rows together to form a block, again taking ¼" seams and matching the seams carefully as you work. Press the seams to one side. Make 35 blocks.

3 For the solid blocks, cut 40 10" squares from a darker blue or indigo fabric.

4 Next, assemble the quilt top. Starting and ending with a nine-patch block in each row and alternating nine-patch and solid blocks, lay out the blocks on a large, flat surface with the following numbers of blocks in each row: 1, 3, 5, 7, 9, 9, 9, 7, 5, 3, 1.

5 Stitch the blocks together in rows, taking ¼" seams. In the longer rows, you will find it easier to match the seams if you stitch the blocks together in pairs and then stitch each pair to another pair, rather than trying to complete a whole row at a time.

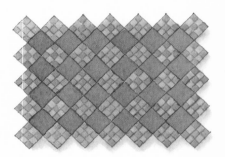

6 Stitch the rows of blocks together as shown in the diagram above. When the quilt top is completed, the blocks will appear to be set "on point."

7 Cut nine 10" squares from dark blue or indigo fabric used for the solid blocks and cut each one in half diagonally. Use these triangles to fill in the gaps around the edge of the quilt top.

8 Cut another 10" square from dark blue or indigo fabric, cut it diagonally into four smaller triangles, and use these triangles to fill in each corner of the quilt top.

9 Using the "top and tail" method (see page 143), attach a 5" single border in red fabric taking a ½" seam.

10 Cut the backing fabric and backing so that they are 1" smaller all around than the quilt top. Assemble the quilt layers, pin, and baste.

11 Mark a simple grid over the nine-patch blocks and a quilting motif of your choice over the solid blocks and quilt.

12 Fold the border over to the reverse of the quilt with a ½" turning and stitch neatly in place, mitering the corners.

LEFT: BOLD SHAPES
The stark simplicity of this
quilt demands an uncluttered
setting that allows the
pattern to stand out.

grandmother's flower garden

The hexagon, often referred to as Honeycomb in the nineteenth century, was one of the earliest designs to be used in quiltmaking. The pattern appeared in *Godey's Lady's Book* (a women's magazine that published many patchwork and quilting patterns for the first time) as early as 1835, and its popularity with quilters has continued unabated ever since.

Because of the need to piece the angles accurately, it is usually done using backing papers—the so-called English paper-piecing method. Newspapers, letters, and even shopping lists were used for the backing papers and, where they have survived, they have proved invaluable to quilt historians in helping to date quilts.

Of the numerous patterns based on hexagons, Grandmother's Flower Garden is almost certainly one of the best known. In this version, each "flower" in the garden has a black center and pale blue or pink "petals." Each flower is then surrounded by white hexagons, so that it almost looks as if the first blooms of spring are poking their heads up through the last of the winter snows.

This pattern is so simple and graphic that it needs very little extra embellishment. Simple outline quilting of each hexagon is enough to give the necessary depth and texture to the design.

grandmother's flower garden

Finished size:
approx. 81" x 79"
Number of blocks: 105

You will need:

FOR THE BLOCKS:
- 105 black hexagons (1½ yds. fabric)
- 360 pink hexagons (1½ yds. fabric)
- 270 blue hexagons (1 yd. fabric)
- 1,260 white hexagons, plus extra to neaten edges (4½ yds. fabric)
- 262 filling-in pieces (1 yd. fabric)

TO COMPLETE THE QUILT:
- ¾ yd. black fabric for border
- ¾ yd. white fabric for border
- 5 yds. fabric for backing
- 5 yds. of 2-oz. batting
- ¾ yd. fabric to make binding
- Matching sewing and quilting threads

All fabrics should be 44" wide.

1 Make a hexagon template with a 1" radius and cut out fabric pieces and backing papers, marking the seam allowance on the wrong side of the fabric. Pin a paper shape to the wrong side of each fabric hexagon, fold over the seam allowance, and baste.

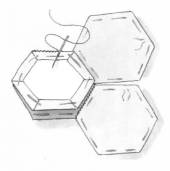

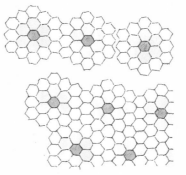

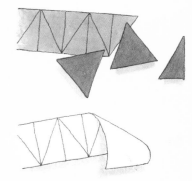

2 To make each "flower" take one black center hexagon, 6 blue or pink hexagons, and 12 white ones. Stitch one pink or blue hexagon to each side of the center and then stitch the side seams, stitching outward from the center each time. Repeat the process, stitching one white hexagon to each side of the colored hexagons, ending by stitching the side seams.

3 When you have completed all 105 blocks, stitch them together alternating rows of ten and then nine blocks, alternating the colors of the flowers. Add extra white hexagons and partial hexagons where necessary around the outside to create a neat, straight edge.

4 To create the dramatic black and white "dogtooth" border, cut strips of black and white fabric 3" wide and mark vertical divisions every 1½". Mark a series of triangles along each strip as shown above, reserving the first right triangle of each strip for the corners, and cut out.

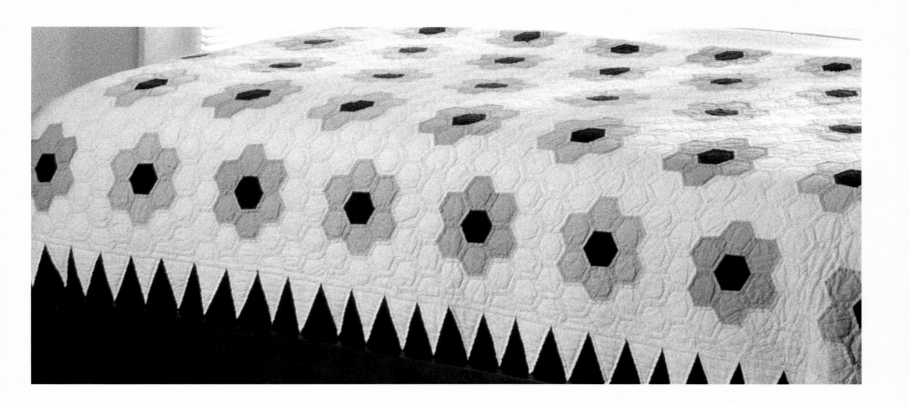

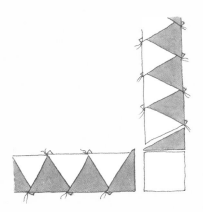

5 Piece white and black triangles together to form parallelograms and then piece the parallelograms to form the border. At the corners, fill in the gaps with the black right triangles cut from the start of each strip in Step 4 and a whole white square.

6 Remove the basting and backing papers. Attach the borders to the quilt.

7 Assemble the quilt layers, pin, and baste. Stitch one line of outline quilting ¼" inside the edge of each hexagon and parallel horizontal lines roughly ½" apart all around the border. Bind the edge.

ABOVE: OUTLINE QUILTING
Outline quilting echoes the crisp, clean lines of the geometric shapes, providing texture without overpowering the pattern.

medallion quilt

This richly textured piece is a triumph of skillful piecing and quilting. In the center of each block is a medallion motif, a variation on a design known as Cogwheel, in which curved blades in alternating light and dark fabrics spin clockwise or counterclockwise, giving a great sense of movement and energy. Each blade comes to a sharp point, making a complex eight-seam join at the center that requires very careful cutting and piecing. This inner circle is surrounded by a sawtooth border in cream and green, whose jagged lines contrast sharply with the flowing curves of the central motif.

". . . Pieced or appliquéd, the quilt has been, in America, a wholly feminine creation."

Quilts: Their Story and How to Make Them,
Ruth E. Finley (1929)

The background fabric and setting squares are a deep blue, while the sashing is a rich, warm brown—an effective use of a contrasting color scheme.

Texture is created in two ways. First, the fabrics: the sashing and background have a slight sheen that contrasts well with the simple cottons used in the pieced medallions. Second, the stitching: simple outline quilting throws the blades into sharp relief, while elsewhere evenly spaced straight lines bring life to what would otherwise be large, empty expanses of solid color.

LEFT: QUILTING FOR EMPHASIS
Contrasts of color and shape are the main key to success in this quilt; the closely stitched lines of quilting also give a dense texture that serves to highlight the simple shapes of the central motif. The wall above displays a quilt pieced from triangles in muted tones that blend perfectly with the restrained décor.

RIGHT: CHANGE THE DIRECTION
Reverse the templates so that
the blades spin in a clockwise
direction on half the blocks
and counter-clockwise on the
others.

medallion quilt

Finished size: 63" x 63"
Block size: 12" square
Number of blocks: 16

You will need:

FOR THE BLOCKS:
- ½ yd. light fabric for blades
- ½ yd. dark fabric for blades
- 1½ yds. light fabric for sawtooth border
- 1½ yds. dark fabric for sawtooth border
- 2¼ yds. blue fabric for background

TO COMPLETE THE QUILT:
- 1½ yds. brown fabric for sashing and borders
- 1 fat quarter blue for background squares
- 4 yds. for backing
- 4 yds. of batting
- ½ yd. blue fabric for binding
- Matching sewing and quilting threads

1 Trace template A on page 157, adding a ¼" seam allowance all around to the outer edge of the curved border. Make four full-size photocopies.

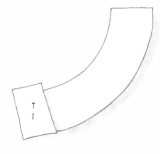

2 Place your photocopy of template A on a flat surface, drawn-side down. Take your first strip of fabric for the sawtooth and center it over the first segment on the photocopy, right-side up. Pin it in position.

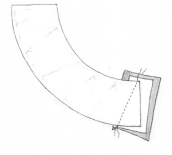

3 Right-sides together, pin your second strip of fabric over the first. Turn the piece over so that the photocopy is on top. Starting in the seam allowance, carefully stitch along and slightly beyond the marked stitching line (see page 72).

4 Turn the piece over so that the fabric is on top and trim the seam allowance to ¼". Turn back the second piece of fabric and press flat. Pin in place. Continue adding strips in this way until the photocopy is covered in fabric. Press and trim the pieced fabric curve and the photocopy underneath to the marked seam allowance. Make another three units in the same way. Remove the photocopies.

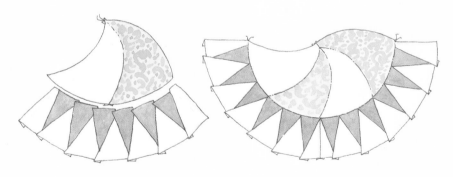

5 Trace template B on page 157, adding a ¼" seam allowance all around. Cut out eight pieces of fabric—four in each color. Machine stitch together in pairs, alternating the colors, and press the seams. Add one border piece to each pair. Make four and press the seams.

6 Stitch together in pairs and press the seams.

7 Stitch together the two halves and press the seam.

8 Cut a 12½" square of background fabric. Turn under the seam allowance on the outer edge of the medallion, center it on the background square, and appliqué it to the fabric. Make 16 blocks, making some of them mirror images so that the blades spiral in the opposite direction.

9 Lay out the blocks in four rows of four. Separate the blocks horizontally and vertically with a 3½" strip of sashing, adding squares in a contrasting color at each corner of each block.

10 Assemble the quilt layers, pin, and baste. Quilt the piece, using a single line of quilting within each individual curved shape of the medallions and closely stitched parallel lines elsewhere to give a good texture. Finish by adding a single border in the blue background fabric (see page 143).

quilting know-how

caring for vintage quilts

Perhaps you own a treasured heirloom quilt that's been passed down in your family for generations—or maybe you've finally tracked down your dream quilt after scouring antique stores and auction rooms wherever you go, or have created your own from favorite fabrics. But no matter how you acquired it, by following a few simple guidelines, you can add years to your quilt's life.

STORING QUILTS

Ideally, of course, you'd like to display your prize possession for all the world to see—but that isn't always practical and you may have to store your quilt for long periods of time.

FLORAL FANTASY
This beautifully executed appliqué quilt combines flowing lines and bold shapes and colors. Note the clever use of small-patterned fabrics, rather than solids, which give a much lighter, airier feel.

● Always store quilts in a dark, dry place. The ultraviolet rays in daylight and fluorescent light break down fabric dyes. Brown and black dyes are particularly sensitive to light, as are delicate fabrics such as silk.

● Always store quilts in acid-free paper, which is available from your local craft store or by mail order, or wrapped in clean cotton sheets or washed, unbleached muslin. Never store quilts in plastics, which contain harmful vapors that can cause the fabric to deteriorate, or wrapped in newspapers or cardboard boxes, which decay rapidly.

● Store quilts either folded in boxes or on storage units, or rolled around wooden dowels sealed with a coat of polyurethane varnish (without varnish, the natural oils in wood may damage the fabric over time) or cardboard tubing covered in acid-free paper.

● If your quilts are folded, unfold and refold them every few months as fabric tends to break down along folded edges. For the same reason, never stack too many folded quilts on top of each other.

CLEANING QUILTS

Many vintage quilts are extremely fragile and cleaning and restoration work should only by undertaken with great caution. However, it is usually safe to vacuum a quilt to remove dust, provided you use a low-suction, hand-held vacuum cleaner with a small brush attachment. Wrap a clean piece of cheesecloth or muslin around the brush, lay the quilt out flat on a clean surface such as a sheet, and work with the vacuum on its lowest setting.

If your vintage quilt must be cleaned, do not under any circumstances take it to your local dry cleaner as the chemicals used in the dry-cleaning process may damage the quilt. Instead, consult a specialist who is used to handling old, delicate fabrics; the textile curator at your local museum may be able to put you in contact with someone who is properly qualified.

Modern quilts can sometimes be washed, but first check that you know what fabrics are involved. Cotton and linen may be washable, but some other fabrics are not. Once you know what fabrics you're dealing with, check that they are colorfast by putting a few drops of water on white blotting paper and gently dab each fabric in the quilt; if any dye runs onto the paper, it is not safe to wash the quilt.

If the quilt is colorfast, then you can wash it. Use a very mild detergent, fold the quilt loosely, and place it in a container large enough to accommodate the entire quilt at one time, such as the bathtub. Gently knead it with your hands, but do not rub the fabric. Drain and add fresh water to rinse until the water runs clear.

Wet quilts are extremely heavy, so get rid of as much water as you can by pressing down on the quilt with your hands. If possible, get someone else to help you lift the quilt out of the tub. Dry the quilt flat on a clean surface, without exposing it to direct sunlight that might fade the fabrics or heat.

REPAIRING QUILTS

Most quilts were made to be used, rather than as show pieces, and so it's almost inevitable that they will show some signs of wear and tear. However, poor restoration work not only looks bad, but it can also affect the value of the piece and, because fashions and methods of fabric manufacture have changed over the years, it can be difficult to find modern fabrics to match the originals. If you're in any doubt about either what needs to be done or how to go about it, consult an expert: many museums have textile conservators and some auction houses and antique dealers may also be able to advise you.

displaying quilts

What's the point of making or collecting quilts if you just fold them up and store them in a closet where no one can see them? Quilts are made to be displayed and enjoyed.

The most obvious thing, of course, is to lay them out on a bed or drape them over a sofa or armchair. Small quilts can also look fantastic draped over a banister or wooden clothes horse. However, some quilts are simply too old or too precious to be subjected to this kind of everyday wear and tear.

Why not treat your quilts as pieces of textile art and hang them on your walls? To make a hanging sleeve, cut a length of fabric the width of the quilt and about 7 to 8 inches wide, stitch the long sides together to form a tube, and stitch the tube to the back of the quilt, making sure you don't stitch right through to the quilt top. Insert a wooden dowel or curtain rod through the sleeve and attach this to brackets or finials on the wall.

Alternatively, separate a strip of Velcro and attach each half to a strip of muslin. Stitch the muslin with the smooth Velcro to the top of the quilt. Glue the muslin with the gripper side of the Velcro to a piece of sealed wood, and nail or screw the wood to the wall.

Very old or fragile textiles may need more protection. Hang a sheet of ultraviolet Plexiglass just in front of the quilt, making sure it does not touch the surface (textiles need air circulating around them in order to stay free of mold and mildew).

LEFT: COLOR CRAZY
The owner of this collection obviously loves bright colors! Crazy quilts in sumptuous velvets mingle with Log Cabin and other traditional patchwork patterns in a vibrant display.

BELOW: RED AND GREEN
The popularity of red and green as a color combination dates back to the mid-19th century, when colorfast red fabrics and thread were first manufactured commercially.

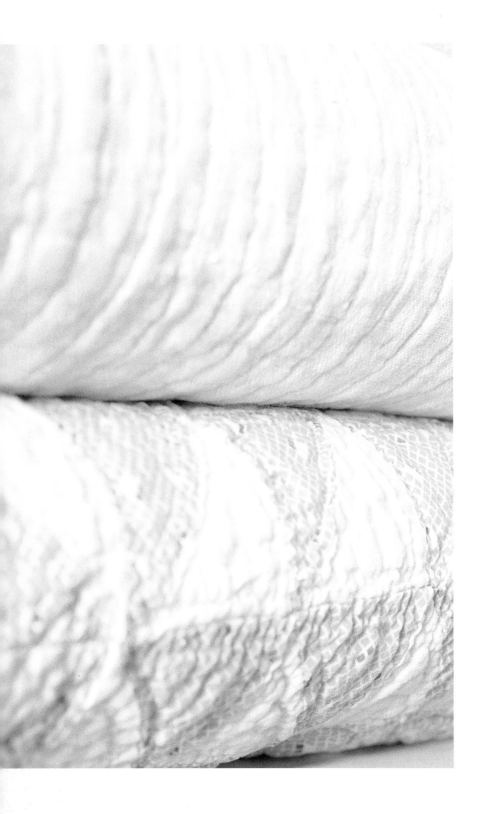

collecting quilts

Most collections start almost by accident: you buy one piece, and then another—and before you know it, you've got a whole stack of them on your hands! You might decide to concentrate on quilts from a specific area, or on a particular pattern or color combination. Ultimately, of course, the best reason to buy a quilt—or any other antique—is because you fall in love with it.

The value of a quilt depends on a number of factors, including its age and condition, its rarity, and how much is known about it. Try to find out as much as you can from the person who's selling it. Is it an old family piece? Does the seller know who made it, or whom it was made for? Where did the maker live? Examine the quilt thoroughly before you buy. Is it soiled or torn? You'll be very lucky to find vintage quilts in absolutely pristine condition, but is the level of wear and tear acceptable to you?

If vintage quilts are out of your price league, why not collect contemporary quilts? Most quiltmakers are thrilled to discover that someone likes their work enough to buy it: do so, and you'll be purchasing the heirlooms of the future.

LEFT: CRAFTSMANSHIP
Simply but beautifully stitched, these quilts would enhance any collection.

RIGHT: THEMED COLLECTION
A collection of mid-19th century appliqué quilts. The stitching varies in quality, but the overall effect is stunning.

techniques

This guide to patchwork and quilting techniques provides a good introduction to the subject and will enable you to make all the projects in this book.

MAKING TEMPLATES

You can buy ready-made templates for many of the shapes that you will need in patchwork, but it is useful (and much less expensive) to know how to make your own.

You will need tracing paper, a pencil, glue, stiff card, a craft knife, template plastic, a metal straightedge or ruler, and a quilter's quarter (or a ¼" wheel if you are cutting a curved template).

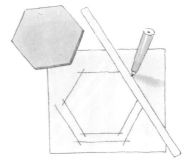
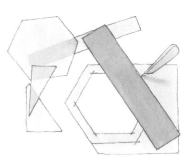

1 Using a sharp pencil, trace the shape onto tracing paper, glue the tracing paper to a stiff card, and cut out the shape.

2 Place the cardboard template on template plastic and draw around it. Position a quilter's quarter (or a ¼" wheel) against the side of the cardboard template, holding both the quilter's quarter and the template firmly so that they do not slip, and draw around the edge of the quarter to mark the seam allowance.

3 Using a craft knife, carefully cut around the inner line on the template plastic. (This will be the stitching line on the fabric.) Then cut around the outer line. (This is the cutting line.)

JOINING TWO PIECES
BY HAND

Joining pieces by hand is a good way to ensure that they fit accurately. With some patterns (particularly curved designs), hand piecing really is the only way to proceed.

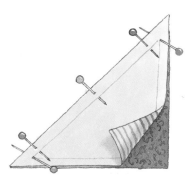

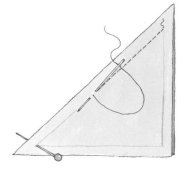

3 When you reach the end of the seam, make a couple of small backstitches to anchor the thread. Press the seam (see page 142).

1 Take the pieces that are to be joined, place the right sides together, and insert a pin through the corner of one piece to the matching corner of the other. Then insert pins along the seam length at right angles to the marked stitching line.

2 Insert the needle on the marked line and make a small backstitch to anchor the thread. Using running stitch or backstitch, sew along the marked line. It's a good idea to turn the piece over periodically as you work, to make sure that the stitches are on the line on both sides.

JOINING TWO PIECES
BY MACHINE

The main advantage of machine piecing is undoubtedly its speed. Also, when you are piecing by machine you do not need to mark the stitching line; just use the guide plate on your machine to check that you are stitching the seam allowance to the right width.

1 Pin the pieces in the same way as for joining pieces by hand.

2 Starting in the seam allowance, place the pieces under the foot of the sewing

machine, aligning the right-hand edges with the guide plate, and start to stitch. Try not to pull the pieces through the machine, as this may stretch the fabric—particularly if it is cut on the bias.

3 Continue until you reach the end of the seam, and make a few more stitches to take you into the seam allowance at the other end. Press the seam (see page 142).

FOUR-PIECE SEAMS

In many patchwork patterns, you start by making units from two pieces and then piece two of those units together to make a larger unit. As a result, you have to deal with several seams—so here's how to get them all to lie neatly, without bunching up and spoiling your pattern.

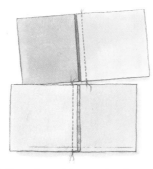

1 Start by taking each of your two-unit patches and pressing the seams in opposite directions.

2 Place the two two-unit patches right sides together. Mark the center seam by pushing a pin through from the back to the front, and pin the rest of the seam as normal.

3 Starting from the center, stitch the units together. Do not stitch into the seam allowance or you will not be able to make a neat seam when the blocks are pieced together.

EIGHT-PIECE SEAMS

Things get a little more complicated when you're dealing with eight pieces instead of four, but the same basic principles apply.

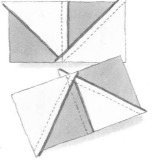

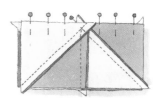

1 Take each of your four two-unit patches and press the seams so that they all fall either clockwise or counterclockwise.

2 Stitch together in pairs, matching the seams.

3 Place the two halves of the block right sides together and push a pin through the center from the back to the front. Place pins at right angles along the whole seam and stitch.

JOINING CURVED SEAMS

A number of the most dramatic and popular patchwork patterns, such as Double Wedding Ring, Fans, Clamshell, and Robbing Peter to Pay Paul involve sewing curved seams, and it's essential that you know how to match the seams correctly. It isn't obvious how to do it: when you place two curves right sides together to join them, you will find that they seem to face in opposite directions so they look as if they don't match at all. To get them to line up, it's a good idea to mark a central balance mark on both of the pieces to be joined when you cut the fabric. Take your time over pinning and basting: this is something that cannot be rushed and you'll find it time well spent.

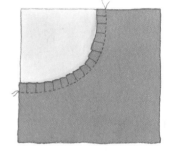

1 Spear the central balance marks with a pin and then put in a pin at right angles to the seam at the very end of each end of the seam. Add extra pins along the seam if necessary.

2 Carefully sew along the stitching line, taking small stitches and making sure you stay on the line.

3 Clip into the curve at regular intervals.

PAPER PIECING

This method, also known as English Patchwork, or English paper-piecing, involves basting a backing paper to the back of the fabric then joining the pieces by hand. It is useful for sharp-angled shapes, as it ensures that each piece is exactly the right size and keeps the fabric stiff enough to allow you to match the corners accurately.

1 Using brown parcel paper or old envelopes, draw around the inner window of your plastic window template and cut out one paper template for each piece of fabric that you are going to piece.

2 Place the plastic window template on the wrong side of your chosen fabric, aligning the grain, and draw around both windows with a chalk pencil or wheel or fadeaway pen. Cut out each patch.

3 Pin a paper template to the wrong side of each fabric patch, making sure it matches up with the inner line. Fold over the excess fabric and baste.

4 Take the pieces that are to be joined, place them right sides together, and whipstitch the edges, taking care not to stitch through the backing papers.

GUIDELINES FOR

PRESSING

In patchwork, pressing means precisely what it says: put the iron down on the fabric and then lift it off again. Never drag the iron across the fabric as you run the risk of stretching the fabric.

● In patchwork, seam allowances are almost always pressed to one side, rather than open.

● If a block has lots of seams, press them all in the same direction. This will help to reduce bulk.

● Wherever possible, press toward the darker fabrics. If you press toward light fabrics, the seam of the darker fabric may show through and spoil the effect of your design. If this isn't possible, then trim the seam allowance on the dark fabric so that it is narrower than that on the light fabric.

● Press seams toward borders or sashing, rather than toward the pieced part of the top.

● Always press the quilt top when you have finished piecing it, as it's impossible to press once the backing and batting are in place.

BORDERS

After you've pieced together all the blocks for the quilt top, you may want to add a border. Not only does this provide a neat finish, it also helps to hold the quilt together visually. There are two basic ways of adding straight borders.

"Top and Tail"

1 Taking a ¼" seam allowance, stitch a border to the top and bottom of the quilt (the short edges, if your quilt is rectangular).

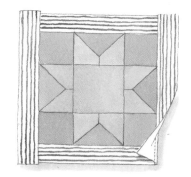

2 Then attach a border to each side, remembering that, because you've now added borders to the top and bottom, the borders on the sides will need to be longer.

"Round and Round"

1 Attach a border to one side of the quilt, letting it overhang at one end by at least the width of the border strip.

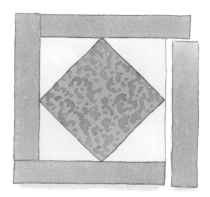

2 Working clockwise around the quilt, add the remaining borders, squaring off the corners if necessary.

MARKING THE QUILT
PATTERN

Once you've completed the quilt top, you should mark on the quilting pattern—before you assemble the quilt layers and baste them together. There are many tools that you can use to mark patterns on fabric—special fadeaway pens, watersoluble pencils, chalk—but whatever you use, always keep your marks as light as possible. The method you use to mark the pattern depends largely on its complexity.

Marking straight lines

Straight lines and grids are probably the simplest of all quilting patterns. They are particularly suitable for intricately pieced tops, where you don't want the quilting stitches to detract from the patchwork design.

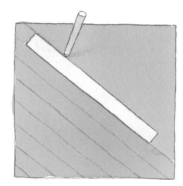

Using a ruler

Decide how far apart you want the lines of stitching to be and draw them lightly on the fabric using a ruler and a graphite pencil, fadeaway pen, or chalk.

Using masking tape

A quick-and-easy alternative is to use ¼" masking tape. Just press it onto the quilt top with your fingertips, taking care not to stretch the fabric as you do so, and then quilt alongside the edge of the tape. But don't leave the tape on the fabric for any length of time as it may leave marks that are difficult to remove.

Using a template

Templates are useful for decorative motifs such as hearts, flowers, or wreaths. You can buy ready-made quilting templates. Alternatively, make your own by tracing patterns from books (or drawing them freehand, if you're confident enough) and following the instructions for making templates on page 138.

Transferring with tissue paper

This method is useful for more complicated motifs, such as interlocking cable patterns, where it might be difficult to cut a template.

1 Trace your design onto tissue paper, place it right-side up on the fabric, and baste along the drawn lines using a contrasting color of thread.

2 Run a pin or needle around the lines to perforate the tissue paper, then gently remove it leaving the basting stitches in place.

3 Quilt the design, and then remove the basting stitches.

ASSEMBLING THE QUILT LAYERS

Once you've completed and marked your quilt top, the next stage is to attach the backing and the batting. You need a large, flat surface big enough to allow you to spread out the entire quilt.

1 Cut out the backing fabric. It should be about 2" bigger than the quilt top on all sides. If you need to join several pieces of fabric to make a big enough piece, place a full width of fabric in the center and add narrower pieces on either side to avoid having an unattractive seam running through the center of the quilt back. Press the backing and then lay it out right-side down.

2 Cut the batting (it should be slightly smaller than the backing) and spread it out on top of the backing, making sure there are no wrinkles.

3 Press the quilt top and center it, right-side up, on the batting—again making sure there are no wrinkles.

4 Starting in the center of the quilt and working outward both vertically and horizontally, pin the three

layers of the quilt together, using special quilter's pins (which are longer than ordinary dressmaking pins) or long safety pins. Insert a pin roughly every 6" or so.

5 Starting in the center and working outward, baste the quilt following the lines of pins and stitching through all three layers. Remove the pins as you finish basting each section. Note: if you're planning to quilt by machine, baste slightly to one side of where the stitched quilting lines will be as it is difficult to remove basting stitches that have been overstitched by machine.

HAND QUILTING

Many quilters still prefer to quilt by hand. Of course, it takes longer—but there's something very therapeutic about the action of hand quilting, and hand quilting definitely has a less mechanical feel to it than machine quilting.

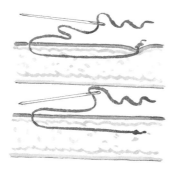

1 Thread the needle with either quilting thread (which is stronger and thicker than ordinary sewing thread, but is available in only a limited range of colors) or with ordinary sewing thread that you have strengthened by pulling it across a piece of beeswax. Make a small knot at one end.

2 With the quilt in a frame or hoop, start quilting from the center of the quilt top, and work outward. Insert the needle a short distance from where you want to start quilting and run it into the batting. Bring the needle up where you want to start stitching and pull the thread until the knot stops on the top. Tug the needle: the knot should go through the quilt top and into the batting, where it will be hidden from view.

3 Work running stitches by inserting the needle down vertically through all three layers, tilting it, and bringing it up on the top of the work. Try to keep the stitches small and even.

MACHINE QUILTING

Guidelines for machine quilting

The advantage of machine quilting is, of course, its speed. It still requires a lot of care and attention, however.

● Use a walking foot on your sewing machine, rather than a general-purpose presser foot, as this makes it easier for all three layers to pass through the machine at the same speed and avoids the problem of the layers puckering.

● Always begin by testing the tension on a sample piece.

● Large quilts are heavy! Roll up the edges so you don't have a huge, unwieldy amount to the left of the area being quilted.

**QUILTING WITHOUT USING
A PATTERN OR GRID**

Apart from elaborate and formal quilting patterns, there are some other options open to you.

● *In the ditch quilting*

This means quilting along the seam lines. In the ditch quilting is a good option when a quilt is intricately pieced or highly patterned: there is no point in quilting elaborate, decorative motifs as they will be lost in the overall pattern.

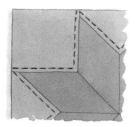

● *Outline quilting*

This means stitching a single line of stitches inside the block or motif about ⅛" away from the seam. The Grandmother's Flower Garden quilt on pages 122 to 125 is quilted in this way. Both this method and echo quilting work well with regular, geometric shapes.

● *Echo quilting*

As you might expect from the name, echo quilting means stitching a series of concentric, equidistant lines around the outside of a patchwork or an appliqué piece to echo its shape. The stitched lines should be about ⅛" away from the shape.

● *Meander quilting*

In this method, which is done by machine, the quilting stitches literally meander their way around in a random, freeform manner. Meander quilting looks most effective when the lines are not overstitched and is a good choice for large, plain areas.

BINDINGS

Binding is the final stage in putting a quilt together. There are various methods, all of which create a neat finish.

Self-binding

In this method, the backing of the quilt is folded over the front and hemmed in place. Alternately, you can fold the quilt top over to the backing.

1 Trim the quilt top and the batting to the required finished size, and the backing 1" to 1½" larger all around. (To fold the quilt top over the batting, trim the backing and batting to the same size and the quilt top 1" to 1½" larger all around.)

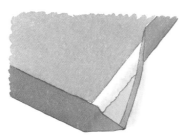

2 Fold the backing to the front, turn the raw edge of the backing under by ½" all around, and pin. Miter the corners and baste to hold in place.

3 Hem using blind hem stitch, or topstitch by machine.

Fold-finishing

In this method, the quilt top forms the edge of the quilt.

1 Trim the batting to the required finished size, the quilt top so that it is the required finished size plus ½" all around, and the backing to the required finished size plus 1" all around.

2 Fold the excess backing up over the batting and pin in place if necessary.

3 Fold under the edges of the quilt top so that they are level with the batting. Slipstitch the edges together by hand or machine stitch through all layers.

Single binding

In this method, a separate binding is attached to the quilt. This gives you the opportunity to use a contrasting fabric that has not been used in either the quilt top or the backing.

1 Right-sides together, pin the first binding strip in position along one long side of the quilt.

2 Stitch it in place, starting and finishing about ¼" from the corners.

3 Pin the next binding strip in place on the other long edge. Stitch in the same way. Trim the long edges so that the binding is level with the quilt top. Fold in the corners neatly and pin.

4 Add the binding to the short edges in the same way.

5 Turn the binding to the back, turn under the raw edges, and pin in place. Slipstitch around all edges to finish.

TEMPLATES robbing Peter to pay Paul (pages 32–35)

This pattern has been reduced to 75% size. Enlarge by 125% on a photocopier to make a full-size template. Add ¼" seam allowances all around when cutting out.

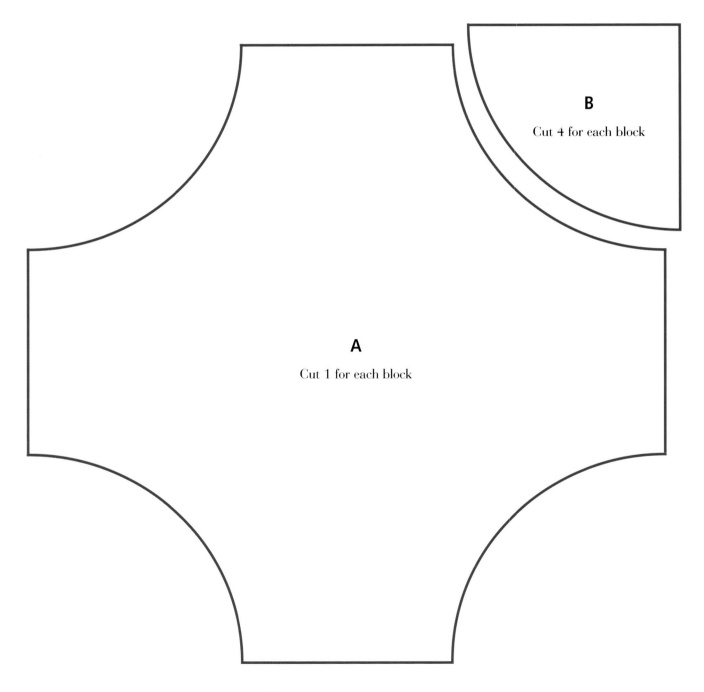

B

Cut 4 for each block

A

Cut 1 for each block

two-color evening star (pages 38–41)

This pattern has been reduced to 75% size. Enlarge by 125% on a photocopier to make a full-size template. Add ¼" seam allowances all around when cutting out.

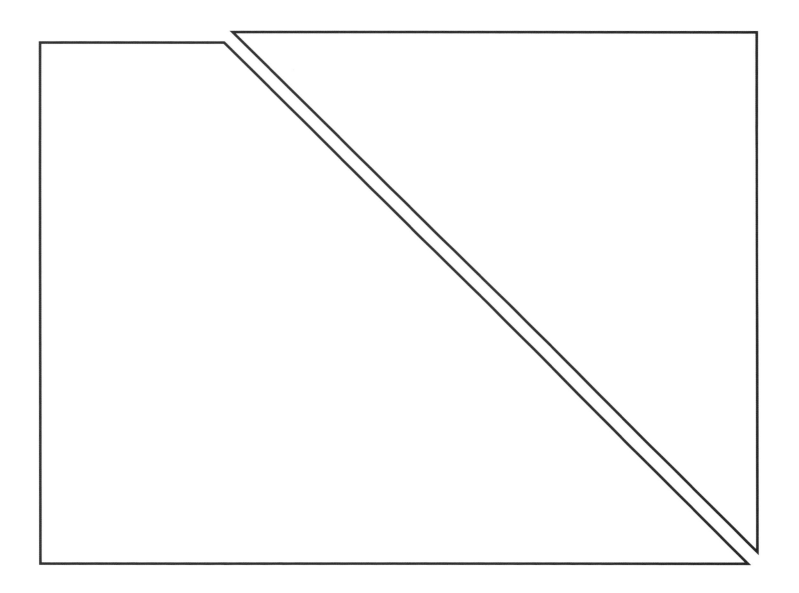

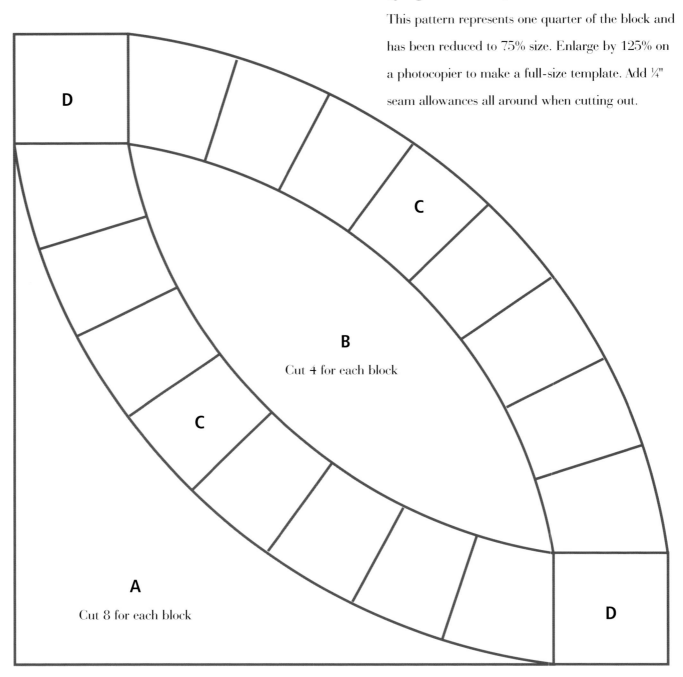

double wedding ring
(pages 70–73)

This pattern represents one quarter of the block and has been reduced to 75% size. Enlarge by 125% on a photocopier to make a full-size template. Add ¼" seam allowances all around when cutting out.

D

C

B

Cut 4 for each block

C

A

Cut 8 for each block

D

tumbling blocks (pages 76–77)

This pattern is full-size. Add ¼" seam allowances all around each piece when cutting out.

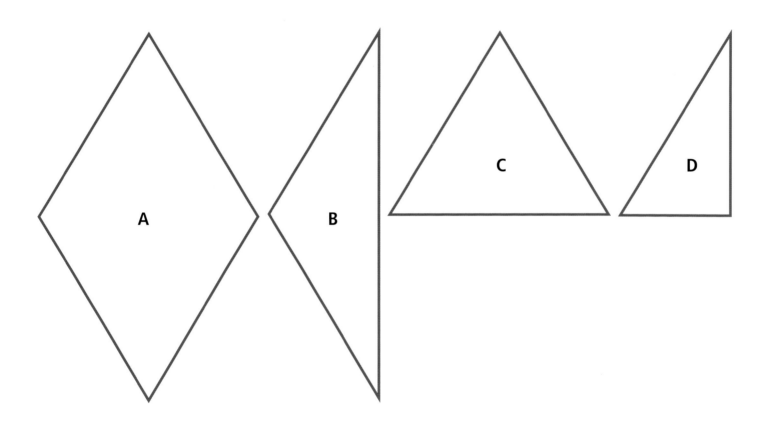

grandmother's fan (pages 78–79)

This pattern is full-size. Add ¼" seam allowances all around each piece when cutting out.

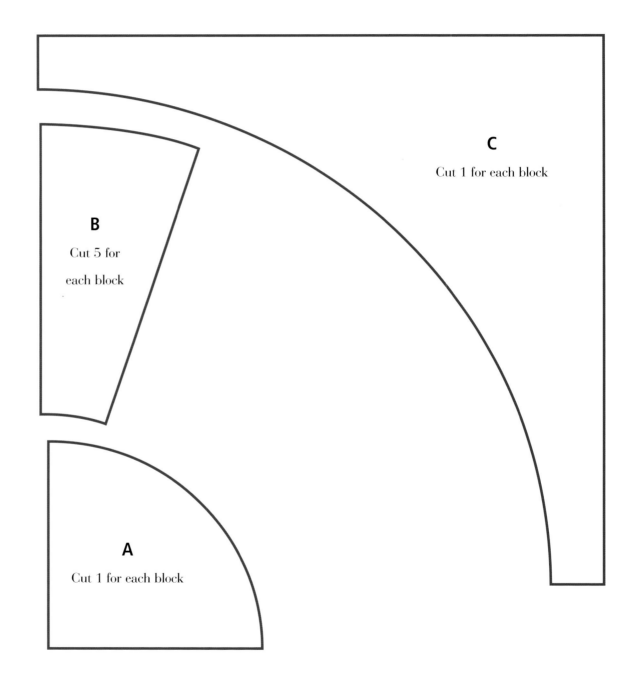

C

Cut 1 for each block

B

Cut 5 for

each block

A

Cut 1 for each block

embroidered fan hanging (pages 88–91)

The templates shown here are 50% of the their actual size. Enlarge by 200% on a photocopier to make full-size templates. Add ¼" seam allowances all around each piece when cutting out.

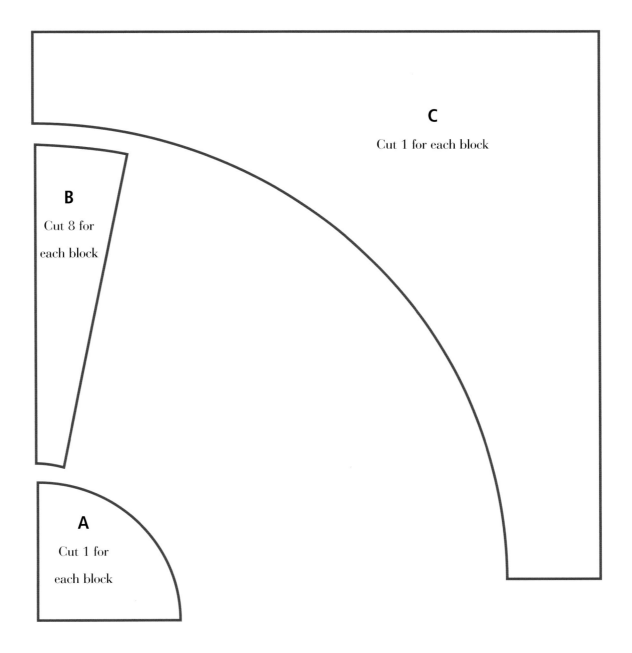

C

Cut 1 for each block

B

Cut 8 for each block

A

Cut 1 for each block

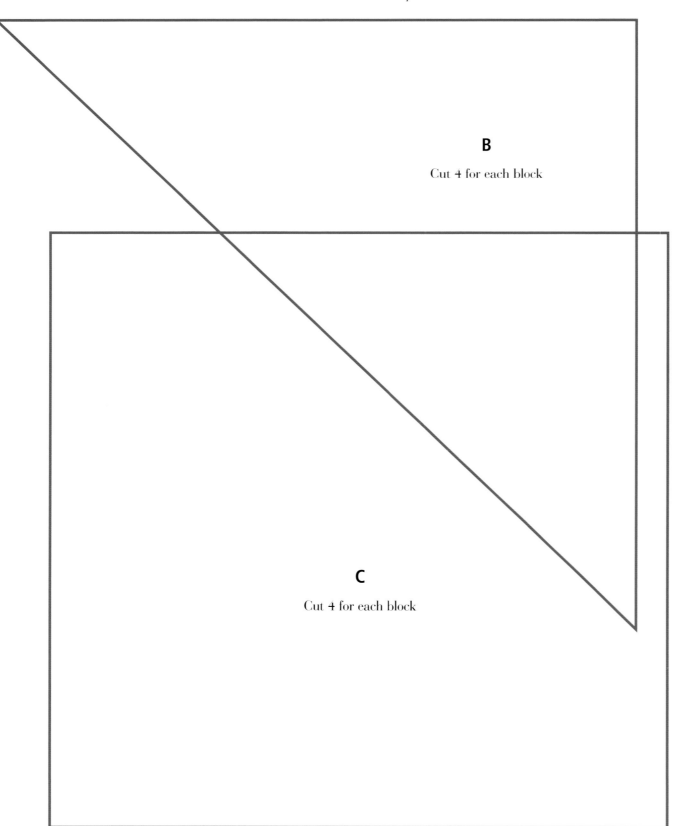

B

Cut 4 for each block

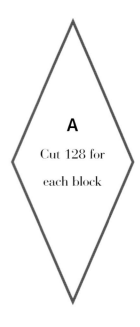

A

Cut 128 for

each block

C

Cut 4 for each block

**stars
upon
stars**
(pages 92–95)

This pattern is full-size.
Add ¼" seam allowances
all around each piece
when cutting out.

medallion (pages 126–129)

This pattern is full-size. Add ¼" seam allowances all around each

piece when cutting out.

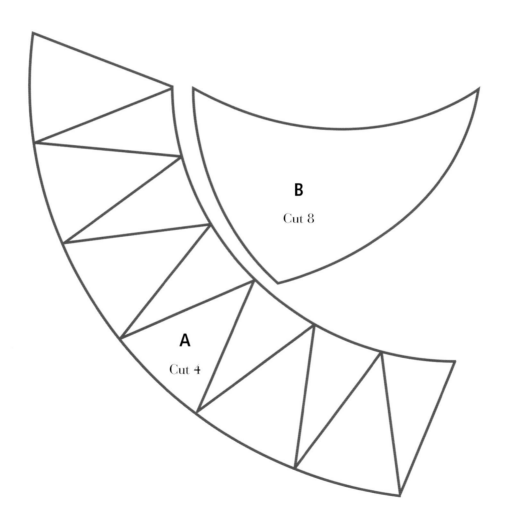

B

Cut 8

A

Cut 4

index

ACKNOWLEDGMENTS

Special thanks must go to Kaisa Mills and Shirley Hibberd for their technical expertise and advice, and to Kate Simunek for her delightful and clear illustrations. At Cico Books, my thanks to Publisher Cindy Richards for asking me to write this book, and to Designer Christine Wood and Project Editor Corinne Asghar for their enthusiasm and help. Last but very definitely not least, love and thanks to Jon for his support, encouragement, and gourmet dinners.